SPECIAL DELIVERY

RANDOM HOUSE NEW YORK

SPECIAL DELIVERY

❀ ❁ ❀ ❀ ❀ ❀

HOW WE ARE RAISING
AMERICA'S ONLY SEXTUPLETS...
AND LOVING IT

BECKI AND KEITH DILLEY
WITH SAM STALL

Copyright © 1995 by Becki and Keith Dilley

All rights reserved under International and Pan-American
Copyright Conventions. Published in the United States by Random
House, Inc., New York, and simultaneously in Canada by Random
House of Canada Limited, Toronto.

Library of Congress Cataloging-in-Publication Data
Dilley, Becki.
Special delivery : how we are raising America's only sextuplets . . .
and loving it / Becki and Keith Dilley with Sam Stall.
p.   cm.
ISBN 0-679-43706-1
1. Child rearing—United States.   2. Sextuplets—United States.
3. Parenthood.   I. Dilley, Keith.   II. Stall, Sam.   III. Title.
HQ769.D463   1995
649'.144—dc20   94-23622

Manufactured in the United States of America on acid-free paper.
2 4 6 8 9 7 5 3
First Edition

Book design by Victoria Wong

*This book is dedicated to Brenna, Julian,
Quinn, Claire, Ian and Adrian. We hope
we are half the inspiration to you
that you are to us every day.*

*In loving memory of Leonor Dilley, who lived
to meet her grandchildren.*

CONTENTS

SPECIAL
DELIVERY

❁ 1 ❁

THE END OF LIFE
AS WE KNOW IT

Their first birthday. The only way we could get them to pose for this photo was to put them inside this toy. (Back row: Ian, Julian, Quinn. Front row: Brenna, Claire, Adrian.)

❀ ❀ ❀ ❀ ❀ ❀

BECKI

The calendar said yes, but my heart said no. On May 25, 1993, I delivered the only sextuplets in the United States ever to survive birth. Now it was a year and a day later. I had returned to The Women's Hospital of Indianapolis with my husband, Keith, and our six children for a reunion with the doctors and nurses who had handled the birth and cared for the babies and me.

It seemed impossible that a year had passed—until I watched the reactions of the hospital staff. The last time most of them had seen the kids, they had been hand-size and supremely fragile. Now they were squirmy twenty-pound toddlers who stared in wonder at the dozens of people gathered around them. Two neonatologists who had helped resuscitate the children after birth each picked up the particular babies they had treated, gazed at them and cried.

All around us, staffers reunited with their tiny ex-patients. A nurse who had worked extensively with one of our sons, Julian, recognized him instantly, even though he'd more than tripled in size since their last meeting. Julian knew her, too, and held out his arms when she picked him up.

Normally Keith and I get nervous when so many people handle the babies, but not this time. We knew they were in good hands, so we allowed ourselves to relax.

We'd done precious little of that during the previous twelve months. When you change an average of forty-four diapers, give forty-five bottles and wash two loads of laundry daily, rest breaks come rarely. With so much to do, it's no wonder that first year was a blur. Plus, in a sense it really *hadn't* been that long. The babies, who were born nine weeks premature, had spent their first three months in the hospital, gaining strength and weight. We hadn't truly felt like parents until we'd finally brought them home. Before that, we'd had to ask permission just to hold them.

Yet watching the staffers get reacquainted with the babies showed us just how far we'd come. Our kids had changed in so many important ways. They'd turned into little people with their own personalities. They played games, got mad and held grudges. They were on the verge of talking. And it had all happened so fast.

Not that we were complaining. It took years of heartache and work just to have this opportunity to walk around all day smelling faintly of talcum powder and sour milk. And after six years of trying to have a baby, including counseling, numberless tests, drug therapy and, finally, a very difficult pregnancy, we savored the chance to get misty over how fast our kids are growing. Fretting that it's all happening too fast isn't so bad when you consider that it almost never happened at all.

❀ 2 ❀

FLASHBACKS

Our wedding day, August 22, 1987. We met at a Wendy's, fell in love and were engaged within a year.

⚜ ⚜ ⚜ ⚜ ⚜ ⚜

KEITH

Considering how our children changed our lives—and the long battle we fought to have them—it's amazing to think that once, long ago, Becki and I actually believed kids wouldn't alter our day-to-day existence very much. We were classic homebodies, preferring hiking through state parks or touring museums to dancing and barhopping. Naturally, we thought packing a kid or two along wouldn't cramp our style at all.

Wrong.

Of course, this revelation didn't come until years after we met, which gave us plenty of time to learn about the other interests and opinions we had in common. Besides sharing a laid-back lifestyle, Becki and I also had similar small-town upbringings. Becki was raised in Ellettsville, a dot on the map near the slightly larger dot of Bloomington, Indiana, a college town that's home to Indiana University. I grew up in Greenfield, just outside Indianapolis. After graduating from Greenfield High School I went to Indiana University to study mathematics and computer science. But while my heart and mind were willing, my wallet wasn't. Covering tuition and expenses was a constant problem that forced me to work lots of jobs. Gradually I found myself spending more and more time at work and less and less time in the classroom. Finally, during 1985, while working at a Bloomington Wendy's, I simply put my college plans on indefinite hold.

At about the same time Becki went through her own transition. After graduating from Edgewood High School she spent a year working as a hair stylist before deciding she wanted to earn a nursing degree. To finance her classwork at Indiana University, she moved back in with her parents and took a job at a fast-food restaurant—*my* fast-food restaurant.

Was it love at first sight? Not really. *Like* is probably more accurate. She was nineteen and I was twenty-two, and we both came to work each morning at five A.M. to get the store ready for its seven A.M. opening. In true hunter-gatherer fashion, Becki was responsible for setting up the salad bar while I prepared the grill and hauled out the day's supply of beef and chicken. Since it usually took only ninety minutes to get everything ready, we often spent the last half hour before opening eating breakfast, reading the paper and talking. I'd even bring in my favorite music and blast it over the in-store sound system (not exactly one of Becki's fondest memories). When we weren't critiquing the tunes (Becki: "This is terrible!" Me: "This is great!"), we dissected current events. Those conversations became the highlights of our days, since intellectual discussions come few and far between when you spend your shift running between the deep fryers and the drive-through window.

And so we became friends—until a few months later, when Becki decided it was time for us to become *more* than friends. Apparently she began plotting this move fairly early in our relationship, when she took me to meet her parents. During the visit her mom pulled her aside and said, "Now that's the kind of guy I'd like you to date. Somebody smart." Ironically, Becki's mom also thought I was "comfortable with my masculinity" because she visited the restaurant one day and spotted me cleaning up the salad bar—in other words, doing something she considered women's work.

Becki's mom may have considered me a smart, eighties kind of guy, but I wasn't clever enough to realize her daughter was interested in me, even though she did everything short of hiring skywriters to let me know. Finally she used a tried-and-true tactic: telling our most loose-lipped, gossip-prone mutual friends that she wanted to go out with me (after swearing them to total secrecy, of course).

In short order one of those friends spilled the beans to me, and that very day I asked Becki if she'd like to see a movie the following evening. As it turned out, I made my move just in time. Becki told me later that if I hadn't asked her out by the end of that week, she was going to approach *me*—quite a step for a small-town girl from a conservative Mennonite family. Her mom had even given her some books explaining how to ask out "that special man."

The next evening I picked up Becki at her parents' house and took her to see *Romancing the Stone*. Afterward we stopped at an all-night diner, ordered two cups of coffee and slid into a corner booth, where we talked until about two A.M. Then we went back to Becki's parents' house and watched TV until it was almost time for her to go to work. Though on that particular day I wasn't due at the restaurant until eleven A.M., Becki was expected at five A.M., as usual.

As morning approached, Becki changed into her uniform and asked if I'd drop her at the store on my way home. By this time she'd already been awake for roughly twenty-four hours straight. Anxious to prove my Sensitive Guy credentials, I announced that, out of sympathy for her sleep deprivation, I wouldn't hit the sack before my shift. I'd like to say I kept that vow, but the truth is I konked out the minute I got home. To make matters worse, Becki worked until four P.M. that day, far past the end of her regular shift, just so we could be together at the store.

From that day forward, we were inseparable. Becki's mom began calling us the Bobbsey Twins. Though we had our first date on January 22, 1986, by that Valentine's Day the handwriting was on the wall: We were going to be married.

Since we had begun looking for rings together in March, my proposal that summer was hardly surprising. I bought the ring—a diamond solitaire on a plain gold band—and decided to pop the question on August 22, when Becki came home from school to share her half-hour lunch break with me at my apartment. I put a bouquet of flowers, complete with a mushy note, in the refrigerator, so she knew something was up the minute she opened the door and began searching for a can of pop. But it still took a while for my "clever" scheme to unfold. I placed the ring, box and all, in one of the holes in an ice-cube tray, then said, in a voice pregnant with meaning, "If I were you, I'd get some ice for your drink."

Becki must have had a tough day in class, because she didn't pick up on it immediately. She said she didn't *want* any ice. Finally, however, after I cajoled her into grabbing some of the ice cubes, she found the ring and I proposed on the spot. Becki thought the whole scheme was corny, but I couldn't see just forking over the ring, dropping down on one knee and saying, "Will you marry me?"

Not that I was able to avoid that traditional—and highly embarrassing—move. As soon as Becki saw the ring and I popped the question, she asked me to do it again on bended knee. Sighing, I knelt and asked once more.

She said yes. After the Big Moment we sat down at the table and ate Doritos and hot dogs and drank Diet Dr Pepper for lunch. Then Becki went back to school, and that was that. Ah, romance.

While we enjoyed a whirlwind courtship, the wedding didn't take place until exactly one year later, to give Becki's parents plenty of time to plan. We held it in a chapel on the Indiana University campus, and everything went smoothly—until I got the giggles. When Becki walked down the aisle, I turned around to look at her and began snickering uncontrollably. Becki's father, who was serving as escort, whispered to her, "What's wrong with him? Slow down." Our wedding album features a photo of Becki, making her way in baby steps toward the altar, looking at me as if I were an escaped lunatic.

Our long engagement provided plenty of time for us to hang out together and discuss the future. During our regular hikes through local parks, we'd often discuss kids. We both wanted them, and the sooner the better. We wanted them so badly that we didn't even bother with birth control during our honeymoon—not that it mattered. We both got such terrible sunburns while touring the Cincinnati Zoo that we wound up sleeping in separate beds for the rest of the trip.

Because Becki made no secret of the fact that she wouldn't mind getting pregnant immediately, her coworkers at Bloomington Hospital, where she had recently begun working as a nurse, started asking if she felt pregnant almost from the day she got back. "I don't know," Becki would reply. "I hope so."

They kept asking for the next six months. And Becki, who doesn't have a very regular monthly cycle, came in for her share of false alarms. She was so anxious that on several occasions she convinced herself she had morning sickness, prompting older women at her hospital to offer their own home remedies. Even her mom dropped regular, not-so-subtle hints, including the classic "Well, I'm ready to be a grandmother anytime." It sounds like a lot of pressure, but it wasn't at the time. We got on with our lives and didn't sweat the fact that we weren't pregnant yet. We figured it would happen when it happened.

But it *didn't* happen, even though we tried for a year and a half. Gradually, the quest became more and more earnest and organized. We bought ovulation prediction kits and conducted basal body temperature tests to time things perfectly every month. And yet, the lack of a pregnancy didn't become an issue until, while undergoing her regular physical during November of 1988, Becki casually told her doctor that we'd been trying to have a child since August of 1987.

The doctor recommended tests for both of us—tests that showed that neither of us had a reproductive system that functioned very well. Each of us, individually, had only a 10 to 20 percent chance of ever having biological children—*if* we had a perfectly functioning partner. But since both of us were in the same boat, fertility-wise, for us as a couple the odds of conception dropped to less than 10 percent. Both Becki's gynecologist and my urologist said we should begin thinking about adoption. "I would suggest at this point that you put your name on an adoption list, take the pressure off and enjoy being married," one of them advised.

But neither Becki nor I was in the mood to enjoy much of anything. The news, which came just as the holiday season approached, hit us like a hammer. For months we hadn't worried about the lack of pregnancy, figuring that having children was our destiny. Now, suddenly, we'd been told that the life path we'd always envisioned for ourselves was forever closed.

Christmas was particularly bad. Every year since we began dating, I had always purchased a commemorative tree ornament for Becki. Though celebrating was the furthest thing from our minds that December, Becki insisted that we had to keep up the tradition. So the day after Christmas we went to the mall and picked through the leftover holiday ornaments for something that fit the bill. We finally settled on a little sleigh that reads, SWEETHEART 1988. To this day, Becki cries when she takes it out and hangs it on the tree.

After the holidays we did as the doctors advised and contacted some local adoption agencies—where we got another load of bad news. The first one informed us that we had to be married a minimum of three years just to make their six-year-long waiting list. We then contacted a county welfare agency, where an employee urged us to consider special-needs children—kids with heavy social, psychological or physical problems. Don't get us wrong, we would have been more than happy to take and love any child that needed us, but this seemed way out of our league. We had no parenting skills to speak of, so we wanted to learn the ropes by starting with a baby or toddler. Plus, we simply didn't have the cash to even consider taking in an older, possibly troubled child.

During the next year, pain seemed to pile on pain. Becki and I had always seen parenthood as a foregone conclusion, and as we faced the numerous roadblocks, lengthy waiting periods and considerable fees imposed on us by the adoption agencies, the stress strained our relationship. To make things worse, three of our good friends had their second children and another became pregnant with her first. When Becki and I were dating and first married, we loved being around friends with kids, because we envisioned ourselves in the same situation soon. But once we got the infertility diagnosis, being around people with kids was like a knife in the heart. Instead of imagining ourselves in their shoes, we saw it as something we could never do.

Consequently, we allowed a lot of old friendships to die of neglect. Becki, though she tried to put on a brave face, found that she simply couldn't deal with baby showers or birth announcements. In some cases she gamely helped plan them, thinking she could handle it. But walking into a store to purchase a shower gift was torture. Frankly, it was hard for either of us to walk near the infant sections of department stores—even though we both felt drawn there. Anyway, when the day for the shower would arrive, Becki always found an excuse not to go, even if it meant signing up for extra shifts at the hospital.

But Becki, at least, made a point of talking about her pain. She even sought out an informal group at her hospital, jokingly called The Infertility Club, whose members were women who had tried to have children for years. Among other things, they told her that having an aversion to baby showers—even feeling an almost unreasoning jealousy toward couples with kids—wasn't all that unusual. Sometimes, they said, you simply have to withdraw from things that cause you grief.

We could have written a book on withdrawal—especially me. Becki and I were both on edge, and after a while we simply stopped talking. She threw herself into her work and classes, and I concentrated on my job. We even began working opposite schedules, so that we almost never saw each other.

We avoided each other because every time we got together it was like fire and matches. Becki generally wanted to speak, at *great* length, about her grief and depression, which was the last thing I wanted to do. I would get quiet, while Becki would cry and insist that we talk. But instead of talking, we argued.

As you can imagine, we weren't exactly the life of the party. In the process of pushing each other away, we also managed to alienate most of our remaining friends and both sets of parents. During those dark days, which lasted from the 1988 holiday season until spring of '89, Becki actually thought we might lose the marriage. She couldn't get past her grief over being infertile, and I couldn't even *talk* about it.

Finally, as the warm months drew on, we reached a sort of accommodation with each other. We decided that one day, somehow, we would become parents, but until that time we would try to make the wait as pleasant as possible—mainly by being good to each other. We decided to spend some serious "couple time" together, going on day trips to Chicago and trading in our four-door sedan for a sportier, two-door model. If we weren't going to have kids right away, we decided, then we might as well enjoy some of the fruits of the DINK (double income, no kids) lifestyle. I bought a computer and we moved from a three-bedroom trailer my parents bought us into a one-bedroom apartment.

It was great. Well, actually, it wasn't *great*, but it was a vast improvement over the previous year. We indulged in every activity that we figured we wouldn't have time for as parents, including pets. Our apartment contained four immaculately kept fish tanks, along with two dogs, an ever-changing lineup of cats and a cockatiel named Elton. Anything that offered the least bit of indulgence interested us.

Still, nothing could distract us for long from the quest to have kids. When our three-year wedding anniversary passed, we began talking to adoption agencies in earnest. Also, Becki read widely on infertility and discovered drugs and treatments that none of our previous doctors had tried or even bothered to mention.

Finally, while we continued pursuing the adoption option, Becki also visited a Bloomington infertility specialist.

Thus began Round 2 of our struggle to have kids. About the middle of every month, Becki would take five days' worth of a pill-form drug called Clomid, which encourages the production of ovulation-producing hormones. After the five days she visited the doctor for an ultrasound examination to see if any eggs were present in her ovaries. If they were, she received a shot of HCG (human chorionic gonadotropin), which encourages the ovaries to release the eggs into the uterus. A day later she underwent artificial insemination (needless to say, my presence was required for this part of the procedure), then went home and waited two weeks to see if she was pregnant.

This got to be old news very quickly. Every month Becki took her Clomid and HCG, and every month produced another disappointment. Even worse, the procedure, which was dictated entirely by her own internal rhythms, began to run our lives. On one occasion I stopped by her hospital so an insemination could be conducted in the middle of her nursing shift. She actually came down to the examination room during her break for the procedure.

Things only got worse after Becki underwent surgery to remove some ovarian cysts and obstructions in her fallopian tubes that inhibited the movement of eggs. The surgery cleared the obstructions, but the doctors told us that Becki would have her best chance of getting pregnant during the following six months, before fresh scar tissue could block the tubes again.

Talk about pressure. Every month Becki would be sure she was pregnant, only to be horribly disappointed when her period arrived. She'd sob inconsolably for hours and then sleep for the better part of the next two days. That's how she coped with depression: Instead of drinking, she slept.

The fact that Becki sincerely thought she was pregnant each and every time just made things worse. She would even have false morning sickness. I particularly dreaded the home pregnancy tests, which Becki always read as positive even though they were absolutely, positively negative. Often I took her to her mom's house to run a second test. I would say it was negative, her mom would agree, and Becki—well, she would *still* think it was positive.

And yet, right in the middle of this terrible, stressful time, something happened that both strengthened our marriage and lifted a huge burden from my shoulders. As I mentioned before, Becki made a point of reading about infertility and talking about it. But I didn't. I couldn't even talk about it to *her*—even though, in retrospect, I should have. The dam finally broke in October of 1991, when we attended an all-day, adoption agency–sponsored roundtable for infertile couples. Though it certainly wasn't meant to, that encounter changed my life.

Basically, we sat in a large room with several other couples and discussed how infertility affected us. This was old hat to Becki, but to me, who had never, ever spoken to another man about the problem, it was a revelation.

It was there, hearing other men talk about the same things that troubled me (but which I had kept to myself) that I realized something truly comforting: I wasn't alone. For years I had thought I was the only man in the world who looked at his wife, who wept at the idea of never having a child, and felt deep, personal guilt about not being able to help. It was that stinging pain, I realized, that had prevented me from talking about the problem, even to Becki.

After that meeting, talking wasn't a problem. We talked all the way home in the car and spent the rest of the day covering territory we hadn't discussed for months. Once we shared our feelings about infertility, we talked about why we had drifted apart and what we could do to make sure it didn't happen again.

It was instant, impromptu marriage counseling. Though infertility was still the biggest crisis in our lives, from that day forward we faced it together.

And there was still plenty to face. Each month's treatment cost around $250, which was quite a stretch for our budget. Occasionally we had to sell things, such as a VCR, to make the monthly bill. Tight finances sometimes forced us to sit out a month—a tough call for Becki, who didn't want to waste any of her postoperation chances for insemination. Whenever we skipped a treatment, she couldn't help wondering if that attempt might have worked.

We wound up spending about fifteen thousand dollars on infertility treatments—enough for a car or a down payment on a house. We wiped out our savings account and cashed in life insurance policies. Becki worked extra shifts and for a while I got a second job. It became such a part of our lives that a nurse Becki worked with compared it to a drug habit. In a weird way, she was right. We had to come up with a certain amount of cash every month, no matter what.

Almost everything in our lives took a backseat to this quest—that is, until the summer of 1992. For the first time, Becki and I took a deep breath, stepped off the treatment treadmill and considered our options. Years earlier we had told ourselves we would someday be parents—it was just a matter of when. This time we told ourselves the very same thing and, for the first time, actually believed it. We decided to quit putting pressure on ourselves and let nature take its course.

How could this suddenly happen, after so many years of tunnel vision and desperation? Part of the change stemmed from the fact that we weren't kids anymore. We had been barely out of our teens when we started our struggle to have kids, but we had grown enough as human beings to realize that it wasn't some sort of death sentence. Also, we had talked to enough infertile couples to know that many do, indeed, eventually wind up with children.

With that hard-won knowledge and maturity, we took a break from the baby chase. We even went on a Florida vacation. We both felt an odd sense of peace, as if something good was about to happen.

Becki felt this particularly strongly. While I was happy just to take a break from the struggle, she insists that from the time of the Florida trip on, she *knew* she would become pregnant before the end of the year. She even thinks the vacation was our unconscious way of preparing for parenthood—one last spur-of-the-moment jaunt before we were tied down with kids. And yet we had no adoption prospects and the Clomid treatments were as fruitless as ever.

Still, we had just purchased a new house, and we had each other. And though there were still disappointments to come, the valleys were never quite as low. By the way, Becki's premonition turned out to be correct. That Florida trip was our last solo vacation before parenthood.

3

JUST KIDDING

Ian. He's a riot.

BECKI

During our quest to have kids, a nurse coworker of mine, Karen, begged me to visit an Indianapolis clinic and try a powerful fertility drug called Pergonal. Clomid stimulated production of the hormone that triggered ovulation, but Pergonal *was* that hormone, in concentrated form.

"You'll get pregnant," Karen said. "You *will* get pregnant."

She badgered me about it for three years, but I refused to listen. I was nervous about using the tricky drug, which required careful monitoring that our Bloomington physicians couldn't provide. Trying it meant visiting a much larger Indianapolis medical center and working with a new team of doctors. We were comfortable with the ones we had, and we liked the smaller, less forbidding Bloomington medical establishment.

There was only one drawback: Our plan wasn't working. We finally accepted that fact after returning from Florida. We tried Clomid a few more times, with the same disappointing results. Discouraged beyond belief, I decided to try something new.

That "something new" was the Indianapolis Fertility Center, the state-of-the-art medical facility where Karen, who had faced her own fertility problems, received help conceiving her two sons. In early fall of 1992, Keith and I drove to the two-story building on the campus of The Women's Hospital of Indianapolis.

Our jaws dropped when we entered the clinic's glass-, brass- and marble-filled lobby. Medically speaking, we were in the big leagues. Here the doctors performed everything from complex in vitro fertilizations to embryo transplants to the latest surgical procedures. We were shown to our doctor's waiting room and sat down next to a woman with a stroller full of quadruplets.

But while many of the men and women at the clinic sought the most complex procedures available, all we wanted was a chance to use Pergonal. And that's exactly what we were given. Dr. David S. McLaughlin, the fertility specialist with whom we dealt, listened to my problems and recommended trying the drug during my next cycle.

The procedure was very straightforward. Each day I would receive a home-administered shot of the drug, then come in for an ultrasound exam to check my ovaries for eggs. If any developed, I would receive a shot of trusty HCG to move them to my uterus for insemination. The odds of Pergonal working on the first try were about 15 to 18 percent.

We also heard about Pergonal's side effects, including a nasty condition called hyperstimulation. In about 5 percent of cases, users' ovaries went into overdrive, growing larger than grapefruits and triggering prodigious water retention. The problem was uncomfortable but usually not dangerous.

There was one other thing: About 25 percent of successful Pergonal users had multiple pregnancies, the vast majority of which were twins. Twins? Well, that would be perfect. "I wouldn't mind having more than one," Keith mused. "As long as it wasn't something ridiculous, like four or five."

If Pergonal didn't work for us, we were told, then we could try more elaborate techniques. But though we didn't mention it at the time, that wasn't an option. Coming up with several hundred dollars each month for Clomid had strained our finances to the breaking point. Given our budget, even more expensive in vitro and surgical techniques were out of the question. It was Pergonal or nothing.

We started the injections almost immediately. Keith gave me a shot each morning before I went to work, and at first he did a great job. He efficiently planted the needle in my backside and withdrew it smartly, with minimal fuss. Unfortunately, he insisted on administering every shot in exactly the same spot. Ouch. After the first few days I worried more about my aching butt than I did about the success of the treatment.

At least we didn't obsess about the process the way we once had. Instead of feeling desperate, I felt quietly confident—so confident that I even mustered the nerve to host a baby shower for Karen, who was pregnant with her second child.

A few days later, I went to Dr. McLaughlin for an ultrasound, which revealed five follicles in my ovaries. That didn't necessarily mean we would have five babies, Dr. McLaughlin quickly pointed out. The odds against all of them successfully transferring to my uterus were high, and the odds against every one of them being fertilized were higher still.

Nevertheless, it was excellent news, though Keith and I didn't get carried away with celebrating. We still had a long way to go to achieve a pregnancy. I received an HCG injection that day and was inseminated the day after that. After the procedure Keith and I went out to eat and drove home. As with previous attempts, there was nothing to do but wait.

A week later, I was briefly hospitalized for hyperstimulation of the ovaries, one of the side effects that Dr. McLaughlin had discussed with us. My ovaries swelled and I retained so much water that I looked several months pregnant.

Upon returning home, I waited until November 22, 1992, to take a home pregnancy test. The night before, my sister and I had bought one. I planned to use it the next day, before anyone got up. If it turned out negative, I wouldn't tell anyone I'd done it. There wouldn't be any crying or three-day funks: I'd handle the disappointment and move on.

After some hesitation I broke open the box, glanced through the instructions and administered the test. It showed positive. Unquestionably positive. A pink dot meant yes, and it was there, big time. There was no mistaking it.

Yet I still didn't trust my own eyes. I woke up my sister and pulled her into the bathroom. "Does this look pregnant to you?" I asked.

My sister gazed groggily at the pink dot, then said in a bored, matter-of-fact voice, "You're pregnant."

"Are you sure?" I said. "Do you really think so?"

"God yes, Becki," she said. "Now will you let me go back to sleep?" And then she trotted back to bed, leaving me alone in the bathroom with my pink dot.

Pregnant. Finally. Thanksgiving was only three days away, so I resolved not to tell Keith until then. But could I hold out that long? I called Karen and broke the news, and she too advised me not to tell Keith until Thanksgiving.

Yes, that was a great idea. In *theory*. But I knew that if I didn't tell him soon, I'd explode. I walked into the bedroom and awakened Keith. He'd worked the night shift at the restaurant and was even more punchy than my sister.

"Honey, can I talk to you?" I said.

"What time is it?" he growled. "Can't I sleep in just one day?"

I kept my composure, pried Keith out of bed, dragged him into the bathroom and showed him the test.

"Yeah, you're pregnant," he said. "Can I go back to bed now?" And then he lumbered off to the bedroom.

Jeez. What's a girl got to do to get a pat on the back around here?

A few minutes later Keith wandered back out, looking slightly less bleary. "Honey," he said, "did you just tell me you were pregnant?"

Finally.

But even then, we didn't let ourselves get carried away. Considering the radical changes Pergonal inflicted on my body, we worried that the test might be a false positive. To confirm the good news beyond all doubt, we visited Dr. McLaughlin's office and checked the levels of naturally occurring HCG in my body. A pregnant woman produces large amounts of the hormone, and I registered a sky-high reading of 3060 (around 100 is normal for a pregnancy).

But to *really* remove any doubts that I was pregnant, the lab had to take another reading a few days later. If the second number was higher than the first, then I was unquestionably pregnant. My sister took me to the clinic on Thanksgiving Day for the second test. By the time we drove home, Dr. McLaughlin's office was already calling with the results. My level had doubled to around 7000.

"So does this mean I'm pregnant?" I asked the nurse.

"Oh yes," she said. "You're very pregnant. And with a level that high we're probably talking about more than one."

More than one? Keith and I immediately thought of twins. I broke the news to our families during Thanksgiving dinner, and for the rest of the evening my mom joyously chanted, "A boy and a girl, a boy and a girl . . ." I was giddy with unimaginable joy—we had so much to hope for.

The Tuesday after Thanksgiving Keith and I stopped by the clinic for another ultrasound to see just how many babies I carried. As the technician passed the sonar probe over my stomach and studied the images it produced, she kept saying "Uh-huh, uh-huh" in increasingly distant, distracted tones. Finally she said, "Becki, how do you feel about multiple births?"

"I think that's great," I replied. "We've been trying for so long. We want twins."

"Uh-huh," the technician said.

"Triplets would be great, too."

"Uh-huh. I'm so glad you're so happy, because right now you have quints."

The words didn't register for a moment. Finally I said, "You're kidding me," but it was obvious from the expression on her face that she wasn't. "Get dressed," she said. "Dr. McLaughlin will want to talk to you."

But first I had to tell Keith, who sat in the waiting room. When he saw my expression, his face fell. "You're not pregnant, are you?" he said.

"Honey," I said, "there are *five*."

Keith turned an alarming shade of gray and slumped against the wall. In a trembling voice he asked for a glass of water and a chance to sit down. I, on the other hand, felt great. I was cruising on a high-octane mix of surprise and euphoria.

After Keith recovered we met with Dr. McLaughlin, who ran down some of the problems we might face. Some of the eggs might resorb into my body in the coming weeks, he warned. And if all five babies survived their first few weeks, it meant a tricky pregnancy both for myself and the kids. The human body, he said, wasn't designed to carry so many children.

Maybe not, but I was game to try. Though we briefly discussed selective termination—aborting several embryos to give those remaining a better chance—Keith and I knew that was not a choice that we would consider. We were delighted to finally be pregnant and looked forward, with hope, to delivering five healthy babies.

Dr. McLaughlin agreed with our course of action, but warned that we faced a very rocky road to parenthood. Frankly, at that moment I was too excited to care. I felt as if I'd already bonded to every one of the babies, even though they were hardly larger than the head of a pin. I called my mom and broke the news, which spread far and wide throughout our families.

Quintuplets were definitely a mind-boggling concept, though the idea quickly grew on me. My coworkers even started calling me Mama Quint. I can't imagine their reaction—or mine, for that matter—if those early ultrasounds had shown the *whole* truth. There were six babies, not five. But we wouldn't know that for a long time.

❊ 4 ❊

LIVING LARGE

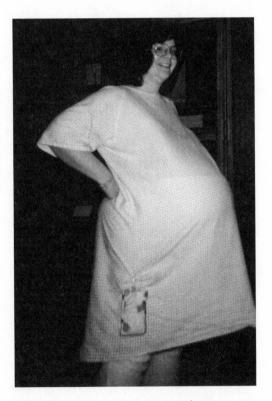

May 15, 1993: twenty-nine weeks pregnant.
(Looks like twenty-nine months!)

❀ ❀ ❀ ❀ ❀ ❀

BECKI

Thursday, April 22, 1993, was not my greatest moment. I had been pregnant for only twenty-five weeks, but I already weighed more than 230 pounds. My doctors at The Women's Hospital of Indianapolis, my home away from home at the time, were afraid the extra mass might cause dangerous blood clots to form in my lower body, so they sent me to a larger nearby hospital for tests.

Though the excursion took only a few hours, it was as thoroughly planned as a camping trip. Because of my fragile condition, I had to travel in an ambulance, accompanied by paramedics and emergency medical technicians. What I *didn't* know was that six uniformed volunteer firemen had been brought in to lift me into the ambulance.

Talk about feeling like a beached whale. The hospital orderlies wheeled me out the main entrance, where my ride—along with a large crowd of onlookers—awaited. The firefighters lined up on both sides of my stretcher, and with a loud "One, two, three— LIFT!" lofted me into the back of the ambulance. Keith offered me a reassuring, "It's okay, honey," then walked out of my field of vision (or so he thought) and broke down in laughter.

That was undoubtedly the emotional low point of my pregnancy. Still, in spite of the discomfort and occasional embarrassment, I can honestly say that carrying six babies wasn't all that bad. Yes, I grew to the size of a full-term mother in only four months, spent the last six weeks before delivery in the hospital and risked contracting a laundry list of life-threatening illnesses, but other than that, everything was fine.

I'm probably playing down the dangers involved, but after struggling for so many years to have kids, I was ready to put up with almost anything to become a mom. I even told my doctors "Don't worry about me. Do whatever will help the babies." I was completely at peace with that. What I didn't realize, however, was how many other trials Keith and I would face in the coming months, from barely avoiding bankruptcy to enduring our first long-term separation, in addition to my seemingly endless string of dangerous medical complications.

Happily, none of these problems hit us at the start of the pregnancy, allowing me a few weeks to enjoy myself. And I enjoyed *everything*. Even stretch marks seemed like badges of honor. When I found my first one, I got so excited that I called Keith at work. "Honey, I have a real stretch mark!" I shouted over the phone. "You have to come home and see it."

Still, even during those problem-free early days we harbored no illusions about the difficulties we faced. For instance, we knew from the start that carrying so many babies to term and delivering them naturally was out of the question. That point was driven home during my ninth week, when I underwent an abdominal cerclage, a surgical procedure in which my uterus was tied shut in order to prevent a miscarriage. The fairly major operation was no picnic, especially since I developed an incredible case of morning sickness shortly afterward. I was often late for work because I got sick two or three times during the drive to my hospital.

Not that I considered this such a terrible burden, mind you. Maybe there's a touch of the masochist in me, but the first day I was ambushed by an unexpected wave of nausea, I ran into the bathroom, threw up—and laughed. I chose to see it as yet another small victory; a sign that my pregnancy was proceeding normally.

After the cerclage I was placed under the care of Dr. Lynda Smirz, the Indianapolis-based ob-gyn who served as my attending physician. Every two weeks Keith and I made the one-and-a-half-hour drive to her office for my examination. In early February, during my seventeenth week, she suggested that I quit my nursing job—a timely idea, since my overtaxed uniform was about to come apart at the seams. I was already slightly *larger* than a full-term mother, which made walking and lifting nearly impossible. Hospital visitors would give me the strangest looks when I told them I wasn't due for another five months. And when I said I was carrying more than one baby, they'd look at my stomach and ask, "How *many* more?"

Though things continued to go well, Dr. Smirz, who read everything she could find about the management of multiple pregnancies, knew the good times probably wouldn't last. There were simply too many dangers. She made a point of never cataloguing every single possibility—for which I am eternally grateful—but I knew the list must have been long and frightening. And these problems weren't just worst-case scenarios, but very real dangers, many of which were entirely out of our control.

Still, I had several points in my favor, including genetics. If I had been five-foot-two instead of five-foot-nine, I couldn't have carried the babies for as long as I did. They would have run out of room. I also enjoyed a considerable amount of good luck. The babies could easily have become entangled in each other's umbilical cords, or their six separate placentas might not have formed normally, inhibiting their growth. None of these things happened, but even the most careful prenatal monitoring couldn't absolutely confirm that. All we could do was try everything we could think of to help the babies and let God do the rest.

As for me, my world seemed to diminish as my size increased. In early March I went on modified home bed rest, which meant that I could only go out briefly. I obtained a HANDICAPPED placard for my car and only visited places where I could sit down and rest, if need be. Trips to the grocery store, for example, couldn't last more than twenty minutes.

But while taking it easy was the best thing for me medically, it did terrible harm to our family finances. Even before I quit work, Keith had lain awake many a night worrying about how we would pay the bills with only one paycheck. He did the math over and over in his head, but the numbers just didn't add up. Once I went on bed rest, the problems began almost immediately. Unpaid utility bills piled up, followed by second notices and, finally, disconnect warnings. In most cases we just stacked the bills neatly and tried to ignore them until we scraped together enough cash to pay.

Keith bore this burden mostly by himself. Though he had visions of bankruptcy court, he rarely shared the true state of affairs with me. I was taking drugs that made me emotionally brittle, and just talking about finances made me cry. The worst part was that we had the money to end our problems, but couldn't get at it right away. Keith and I had both cashed in our life insurance policies, our tax refund was due and I was expecting medical disability insurance payments, but none of this would arrive for two months. Meanwhile, we somehow had to pay double or triple our usual expenses with half our usual income.

To make ends meet we sold one of our cars, along with anything else that seemed valuable. But it wasn't nearly enough. On top of everything else, we ran up a higher-than-necessary food bill because my morning sickness made me extremely finicky. The only thing I could keep down was—get this—fast-food burritos. But after weeks of this budget-breaking diet we learned that the particular restaurant Keith frequented had been implicated in a citywide hepatitis outbreak. I called the local public health office to find out if I might be infected, but the list of symptoms reeled off by the staff nurse wasn't very helpful. "Are you feeling bloated?" she asked. "Are you experiencing nausea?" Well, yes, but I doubted it had anything to do with hepatitis.

It turned out I wasn't infected, which was about the only piece of good news we got during those dark days. Things got so bad that Keith, who kept our accounts on his computer, offered to put a secret password on the files so I couldn't upset myself by looking at them. Our parents helped us as much as they could, even as both were dealing with tough financial problems nearly as bad as our own.

Though we became so desperate that we sold anything that wasn't nailed down, Keith wouldn't hear of me parting with my engagement ring. But as the weeks wore on and we faced the very real danger of losing our electricity, gas and phone in the middle of an uncommonly cold Indiana winter, I knew what I had to do—whether or not Keith approved. Not that it was any easier for me than him. I remember thinking that I was selling a promise—a promise that Keith and I would get married. But my mom told me that our life together wasn't what sat on my finger; it was what was growing inside me.

Accompanied by a friend, I finally summoned the courage to waddle into a very nice jewelry store and sell the ring. I took off my ⅓-carat solitaire ring, which I considered the most beautiful ring in the world, and laid it on the counter. The clerk looked at it and said, "I'll give you seventy-five dollars for it."

I thought I had misunderstood him. "That can't be," I said. "I know my husband paid so much more than that."

"Then he got taken," the clerk said. "If it's important to you for sentimental reasons, put it back on your finger. But that's what it's worth."

But seventy-five dollars wasn't enough. I took off an emerald ring Keith had given me for my birthday and offered that one, too. The clerk tacked on another twenty-five, giving me an even hundred dollars. I was so devastated that all I could say was "Take them." As we left my friend put her arm around me and said, "You did it for your children. You did it so you could have a family." Keith, when I finally told him, was just as mad as I thought he'd be, but in the end I think he understood.

While our personal life fell to pieces, the pregnancy sailed along beautifully. I was taking a drug called Terbutaline, which both quiets labor pains and relaxes the blood vessels feeding the placenta, promoting faster fetal growth. In mid-March I reached the twenty-week midpoint of the pregnancy without any complications worthy of the name. I felt so good that I let my mom, my sister and a pack of friends take me to an Indiana University production of *Hair*. I didn't know it at the time, but this would be my last public appearance until after the kids were born.

Getting dressed was almost as big an adventure as the trip itself. Almost all my maternity clothes were too small and I had to struggle to find a pair of shoes that fit. At the auditorium I was seated on the aisle to accommodate my many trips to the bathroom. During the finale the cast grabbed audience members to dance with them onstage, and one young actor made the mistake of approaching me. The poor fellow. When I stood up his eyes almost popped out. I went onstage and danced while my family and friends rolled with laughter.

During the next two weeks I started feeling sporadic contractions (a fairly common problem for mothers of multiples) that were countered with increased doses of Terbutaline. The drug, however, caused me to gain water weight so rapidly that I put on eight pounds over the next two weeks, forcing me to outgrow the last of my clothes. From then on, it was nightgowns or nothing.

The Terbutaline created plenty of other problems, including shortness of breath, palpitations and panic attacks. For the first twenty to forty minutes after taking a new dose I would climb the walls, complaining that it was too hot, I couldn't breathe and I had to go outside. Keith must have drawn on some inner reserve of patience to cope. "You can't do that," he would say. "There's snow on the ground and you're in your nightgown." He tried to be home as much as possible whenever I was in the throes of the drug.

Sometimes I think he birthed these babies as much as I did, because every crisis I faced, he faced too. Thanks to his evening work schedule, he was home all day in case of an emergency. That arrangement also made life easier for him. If he'd been at home with me at night there would have been nowhere for him to sleep, because I took up both sides of our queen-size bed.

Every night before he went to work, Keith tucked me in. It was a bigger operation than one might imagine, since it took so long for me to get comfortable. First he'd place several pillows under my legs and stomach, then more behind my back to raise me to an upright position, so I could breathe. Then he'd give me a full-length pillow to hug and cover me with a blanket or two, depending on the weather. This got to be such a habit that to this day I can't sleep unless Keith tucks me in—though these days it usually consists of a kiss on the forehead and a quick "You're tucked in." We'll probably do this until we're eighty.

As spring approached, our finances gradually improved. The money from the life insurance policies arrived, our tax refund turned up and my medical disability insurance came through. Suddenly we had enough cash not only to pay off most of our bills, but to set aside a small reserve for the next several months. It was such a sense of accomplishment. I remember we celebrated by going to the grocery store and getting a huge load of supplies. We were sitting comfortably—until the very next day, when I went into premature labor.

It was April 15, and Keith and I had gone out to dinner to celebrate. As we sat in the dining room I began to feel cramps, but they were the same sporadic pains I'd felt for weeks, so Keith went to work as usual that evening. But as the hours passed the pain grew more severe and regular, increasing my nervousness. Finally I called Dr. Smirz's office and was told to come to The Women's Hospital right away. As soon as Keith got home we drove to Indianapolis, never realizing that I wouldn't return to Bloomington for three months.

The gravity of the situation hit Keith as soon as we reached the hospital. While I was wheeled off to a room, he filled out the admissions paperwork, including a consent form for an emergency caesarean section. For the first time he realized that the babies could be born that day.

Not if the hospital staff could help it, however. The babies, who weighed less than a pound each, were only twenty-four and a half weeks old, giving them almost no chance of survival.

Somehow they had to reach at least twenty-six weeks, when their lungs would begin to function, so that ventilators, machines designed to assist breathing by forcing oxygen in and out of the lungs, could be used. That single step would increase their survival chances to perhaps 60 or 70 percent.

At first, however, I wasn't too worried. For one thing, my labor pains, far from being the unbearable agony I expected, didn't seem to hurt enough to be dangerous. But this was a false comfort, I soon learned. Carrying six fetuses had stretched my uterus to the limit, making it incapable of generating powerful spasms. I could never feel the intense contractions other women experience when having a single child. As a matter of fact, that very evening I was awakened from a sound sleep by a team of nurses who told me I was in full labor—and I was sleeping right through it. I was immediately placed on a very powerful labor-inhibiting drug called magnesium sulfate.

Given my unstable condition, it was decided to keep me at the hospital for the rest of the pregnancy. The magnesium sulfate slowed down the labor, and me along with it. My speech became slurred, my reflexes deteriorated and my energy drained away. Keith, who phoned constantly when he wasn't at the hospital, soon learned that long pauses in our phone conversations meant that I had nodded off. Whenever this happened, he would wait a few moments, then shout, "Becki, are you awake?" Usually, provided the receiver hadn't fallen too far from my ear, I'd revive and say, "Yeah. What was I saying?"

It was a frightening time, especially since I was so far from home. But my grandmother, as soon as she heard I was hospitalized, began something called a "prayer chain" among her Mennonite friends. She asked them to pray for me, and they passed along the request to other churches and individuals.

They did a lot more than pray. I received buckets of letters, cards and small gifts, most from total strangers. Just opening the mail kept my mind off my troubles. At the time I wanted to write everyone back, but thanks to the magnesium sulfate I could barely form a clear thought.

Some of the most interesting packages were from people who sent me coupons for diapers or baby shampoo. In the midst of raiding the newspaper for their own shopping trips, they had actually remembered a pregnant woman in a faraway place that they would probably never meet. I got mail from people all over Indiana, most of whom said their churches were praying for me. It was a very warm feeling. I still felt lonely, but I never felt like I was *alone*.

The magnesium sulfate was causing me unending trouble, because in addition to putting me to sleep, it also speeded up my water retention. During my first couple of weeks in the hospital I gained as much as four pounds a day, prompting fears that the excess fluid would settle in my lungs and trigger respiratory collapse, or else bear down on my chest cavity and cause heart failure.

Instead it collected in my feet, knees and hips, which meant that it wouldn't hurt me, just make my life difficult. The fluid pushed my internal organs, including my lungs, upward, making it hard for me to catch my breath, especially while lying down. At night, just as at home, I sat up straight in bed on a pile of pillows to keep from gasping. But I could never get the pillow arrangement quite right, because the expert, Keith, often wasn't around to help me. Daytime wasn't much better, because my personal water reservoir got so large that I couldn't keep my balance while walking. If I wanted to get around, I had to shuffle sideways or backward, or have someone push me in an extra-large wheelchair.

While I struggled to walk, my doctors struggled to determine their next move. Though they recognized the need to get the babies up to, and hopefully well past, twenty-six weeks, I obviously couldn't stay on the magnesium sulfate for long, given the side effects. During one two-day period I put on thirteen pounds.

I was finally placed on a powerful diuretic—a risky move for a pregnant woman, since restricting one's water supply can inhibit blood flow to the fetuses. In this case, however, carefully monitored doses kept me from swelling further, carrying me past the magic twenty-six-week mark.

Though no one turned cartwheels when the big day arrived, things began looking up after that. The magnesium sulfate was discontinued and I was placed on a device called a Terbutaline pump, which automatically gave me smaller, carefully monitored doses of the milder labor-inhibiting drug I'd used at the start of my pregnancy. The water retention, while it never quite went away, at least lessened. Best of all, I could once again walk forward.

At twenty-eight weeks I was allowed to get out of bed and walk around much more often—another calculated risk. Because I'd spent most of my hospital stay lying down, there was a chance I'd develop blood clots that could seriously injure or kill me. When you sit as much as I did, the blood moves sluggishly through your pelvis and legs—especially in my case, since I had half a dozen babies pressing down on those areas. That lack of movement causes clots, which can slowly travel to the lungs or brain, where they can result in a stroke or respiratory failure.

To counter the problem, I got two shots a day of blood thinner and permission to take brief walks down the hospital hallways. I must have had a serious case of cabin fever, because when Dr. Smirz told me I could take a stroll, I immediately strolled to the elevator, headed for the lobby and explored the hospital gift shop.

When I was finally apprehended, I said she *told* me I could go for a walk. She just didn't say how far.

The hospital staff, Keith and I had all breathed sighs of relief when the babies passed twenty-eight weeks. But at thirty weeks, everyone began to get nervous again. Dr. Smirz worried that the longer we waited before delivering the babies, the greater the chance that something drastic might go wrong. Everyone looked for the first signs of a severe problem. "If you sneeze funny, we deliver these babies," Dr. Smirz told me.

We had plenty of unknowns to worry about, since the babies couldn't be monitored as carefully as we would have liked. Only later would we realize how badly those unborn kids conned us. Even with weekly ultrasounds, no one (me included) ever noticed that there were six babies instead of five. That's not as surprising as it sounds, considering just how grueling those ultrasound sessions could be. While a woman with only one child can expect to spend perhaps fifteen to twenty minutes lying on the examining table, my sessions lasted three hours or more.

Ultrasounds became an endurance test for both me and the technicians, who often took their lunch breaks early so they could concentrate on me. First I would lie down on the table, forcing all the babies to roll up on my lungs, nearly suffocating me. Then the technicians, who designated the babies A,B,C,D and E, would run the ultrasound probe over my stomach, trying to distinguish one child from another from among the mass of arms, legs and heads that appeared on their grainy, black-and-white video monitor. They wanted to measure head circumferences and body sizes to make sure everyone was growing at the right speed, but sometimes they couldn't tell which head belonged to which body.

This unavoidable problem gave the doctors trouble, because any gaps in the coverage of a particular child could mean that a birth defect or growth problem might be missed. Of course, since they assumed there were only five babies, someone *did* go unmonitored during every exam. Thankfully, it likely wasn't the same baby each time. The technicians probably looked at various combinations of kids throughout the pregnancy, meaning there wasn't one "stealth" child that they kept missing. I even remember them complaining about the kid on my upper left side, saying he had an attitude problem because his heartbeat was so hard to monitor. In retrospect, they were probably trying to sort out the heartbeats of two different babies.

If the procedure was tough for the technicians, it was extremely difficult for me. Ultrasounds have to be done on a full bladder, which for some reason improves the sonar images. This meant I got to spend one afternoon each week lying on my back, barely able to breathe and fantasizing about the ladies' room while a technician pressed a largish object down firmly on my nether regions. To add to the hassle, the babies for some reason got very rambunctious during exams, driving the technicians to distraction with their continual scooting around.

It would be nice to say that in spite of what the doctors told me, I always had some strange, mystical feeling that I carried more than five babies. Well, I didn't. Never during the pregnancy did I have the slightest inkling of the true situation. Once, when a nurse who was checking the babies' heartbeats announced that she couldn't find "Baby F," Keith and I both rolled our eyes and reminded her that there were only five. Afterwards Keith said, "Can you imagine? Six?"

But though I feel slightly guilty about not somehow knowing, I've also come to realize what a gift ignorance was. Sextuplets were uncharted medical territory. If the doctors had known the truth they might not have been as optimistic, and I would have been more frightened. But quints were another matter. Dozens of women had carried them successfully, and everyone knew it could be done. That gave me a sense of security that would not have existed if I had known the true state of affairs.

As the final days of the pregnancy approached, I filled out to my maximum weight of 280 pounds. One of the best parts of Keith's visits was watching his face when he first walked in the door and saw how much I'd grown during the week. His eyes would glaze over and he'd mumble, "Oh my God." I used to look at myself in the mirror before he arrived, trying to imagine his reaction. Once I asked the nurses if I should stick some pillows under my gown to *really* freak him out, but they shook their heads and said, "Honey, don't bother."

I got so large that I couldn't turn around in my room's shower stall. I had to wash one side, step out, turn around and go back in. My stomach formed a convenient shelf for both my meal tray and the TV remote control—though the babies sometimes kicked so hard that they knocked the remote to the floor. I was supposed to wear a pair of support hose to help keep blood from pooling in the lower half of my body, but when I put them on it felt like an anaconda was swallowing my legs. Plus, I was so large that I couldn't get them on without help, and that's a tough thing to ask of someone. Let's just say I didn't wear the hose any more than I had to.

My long days of bed rest got to be quite tedious. Afternoons were the worst. I had the option of watching TV, but I'm not a soap opera fan and the hospital's closed circuit movie channel showed the same four or five movies all month long. Over the course of the pregnancy Keith and I watched *Wayne's World* and *Beauty and the Beast* so many times that we can still recite entire scenes.

Thankfully, I had a rather large project—picking names for the kids—to occupy my time. I began compiling gigantic lists of boy and girl names almost immediately after learning I was pregnant, which Keith and I slowly whittled down. Keith insisted on several rules. The names couldn't sound like we stole them from soap operas (which nixed handles like Spencer) or be painfully trendy, like Dakota. Keith rejected the name Quentin Everette because he thought it sounded perfect for an eighty-year-old man, but not a toddler. We wanted basic, down-to-earth names that hadn't been overused. While I was hospitalized I toyed with seemingly endless first and middle name combinations, occasionally calling Keith to ask him what he thought of, say, Ian Michael.

Our biggest dispute arose over Bronwyn, an old Scottish moniker that I loved and Keith loathed. "I hate Bronwyn," he said. "It sounds like someone clearing their throat." I told him we could call the baby Brenn or Brenna for short, and he finally suggested that we just *name* her that. And so Brenna made it onto our list of finalists: four first and middle name combinations for the boys and four for the girls. After months of haggling, that was all we could agree on. It's a good thing we didn't have a fifth son, because we would have had nothing to call him.

Such distractions came in handy, especially since Keith couldn't always be around to cheer me up. Not being together was the worst part for me. Before I went to the hospital we had never spent so much as a night apart. This was a *big* separation, and seeing each other only once a week made the rest of the week tougher.

Keith was also the only person I could share bad news with. I didn't want to worry either my mother or his, and I didn't want anyone to know how scared I really was. I tried to be the brave lit-

tle trouper for everyone else, but it was Keith I called in the middle of the night to say, "I can't take it."

Naturally, I lived for his weekend visits. My nurses went above
and beyond the call of duty on those special days, helping me do
my hair and apply makeup. It really gave me something to look
forward to. During his stays he slept on a hideaway bed in my
room, and the hospital gave us lunch and breakfast.

Keith also came bearing gifts. I was on a strict low-sodium diet,
and my rations of bland breakfast cereal and saltless dinner
entrees made high school cafeteria food look enticing. During his
visits, Keith would "supplement" this lineup by smuggling in an
occasional hamburger or box of Chinese carryout under his
jacket. Sweet and sour pork was the best.

Sometimes he would even visit me at the end of a weekday
shift, spend the day at the hospital and then drive back to
Bloomington in time for work that night. When he wasn't
around, we'd keep in touch through *very* frequent phone calls.
It's a good thing our finances were straightened out by that time,
because several months our phone bills topped $500. I'd also
entertain other visitors, especially my coworkers from Bloomington Hospital. It was so cute, because when they saw me they
never knew quite what to say. Most of their responses fell along
the lines of, "Boy, you're sure *big*."

The nurses became my surrogate family, stopping in to visit me
during slow spots in their schedules. One even gave me flowers at
the beginning of each new week of the pregnancy. All that attention was comforting, especially since, being a nurse myself, I
knew just enough about the specialized world of obstetrics to
frighten me. Yet there were some practical advantages to being
hospitalized. When I lived in Bloomington I would find some
medical issue to worry about and then fret until I could bring it up

at my next doctor's appointment. At the hospital, medical experts could end many of my fears immediately with a quick test or examination. The nurses also checked the babies' heartbeats once every shift, and they let me listen, too. It got to be such a routine that they drew Xs on my stomach over the best spots to hear particular babies.

But such distractions aside, I must admit that as I approached my thirty-first week, I got more and more anxious. Frankly, I was tired of being pregnant and ready to be a mom. Dr. Smirz was equally worried, waiting for some sign that things were going wrong. The minute they did, an elaborate plan would swing into motion.

The hospital prepared for the birth for weeks. The Women's Hospital isn't very large, which meant that in some departments almost the entire staff would be needed for my caesarean section. Two operating rooms were reserved for the roughly thirty people involved in either the surgery or life support for the babies, and all of the participants wore pagers twenty-four hours a day so they could assemble quickly when the Big Moment arrived.

As the end of May approached, everyone knew that day wasn't far away. It couldn't come fast enough for me. I remember that on the Monday of my last week, I felt incredibly blue. I had just heard babies crying in the nursery, and the sound filled me with an almost desperate longing. I wanted to see *my* babies—immediately. I wanted to hold them and feed them. When Dr. Smirz stopped by I shared my mood with her. "I'm ready for this to be over," I said.

But Dr. Smirz, who knew that every day the babies spent inside me improved their chances for good health, offered a pep talk instead of a shoulder to cry on. A while earlier the two of us had decided to go for the record for the longest gestation of quintuplets (thirty-two weeks and four days), and she reminded me that we weren't anywhere near that mark. Amazingly, after our chat my depression lifted and I felt gung-ho again, ready to carry the babies till doomsday.

My physical condition seemed to match my upbeat mood. During those closing days I felt better than I had in weeks. I was shedding water weight to the tune of eight pounds a day. It was great: Eat anything you want and still get up in the morning and be 8 pounds lighter.

On the morning of May 25, 1993, I awoke at the crack of dawn, ready to see my mother and sister, who were coming for a noon visit. For breakfast I received my typical low-sodium fare, cream of rice. I became impatient with myself while eating, because for every bite I maneuvered into my mouth, I seemed to spill an equal portion down the front of my gown. I couldn't make my mouth do what I wanted it to do. Finally, disgusted, I walked into the bathroom to brush my teeth. But when I looked in the mirror, I saw that the entire right side of my face had gone slack and numb.

I didn't know it yet, but the sign had come. It was time to see the babies.

❦ 5 ❦

HOME ALONE

(The mighty) Quinn

KEITH

Toward the end of her pregnancy, spending time with Becki was like living a scene from the movie *Alien*. I'd sit in her hospital room for hours, staring in amazement at her stomach as it moved back and forth with little bulges that we knew must be heads, feet and arms. All moms-to-be feel their babies kick, but this was like watching a soccer scrimmage.

One evening as we watched TV at the hospital, I noticed an unusually large, hard bump just below her ribs. "Becki, you've got some kind of mass," I said. "We've got to get a doctor in here."

We quickly found a nurse, who leaned over to examine the bump while we waited anxiously for a verdict. "Oh, that's not a mass," she said, scolding us. "That's a *butt*." She gave it a firm push and it promptly vanished, never to be seen again.

Oh, of course. Someone's butt. Sorry I asked.

It seemed like I was always getting blindsided by such medical oddities—especially during the weeks Becki stayed in the hospital and I lived by myself in Bloomington. While Becki could fall back on her nursing training and seek answers from the experts around her, I was usually on my own. Because of that, many of the ups and downs that she took in stride absolutely floored me.

There wasn't much I could do about it. I still worked at the very same restaurant where we had met, though I was now assistant manager for the evening shift. We needed the cash to cover our expenses, so when Becki went off to Indianapolis I continued working five or six days a week, from around six P.M. to four or five A.M.—however long it took to clean up the store after closing. Then I'd head home in the wee morning hours to our cat, Ed; our Welsh corgi, Winston; and two tanks full of fish. Usually I watched a couple of hours of bad TV, talked to Ed and Winston (they never talked back) and hit the sack.

Not that I spent every single evening channel-surfing or holding one-sided conversations with my pets. During those weeks of forced bachelorhood I also struggled with an array of wrenching changes that transformed our carefully thought-out postpregnancy life.

In the beginning, we had had a plan. We had decided very early in the pregnancy that after the kids were born, Becki would return to nursing while I became a full-time house dad. This was no great sacrifice for me, since I'd flipped enough burgers for two lifetimes, thank you. It also made practical sense, because Becki could pull down around $25,000 a year while working only three 12-hour shifts each week, leaving her free most of the time to help with the babies. Becki's parents, who lived in Bloomington, could also lend a hand. Her mom even volunteered to retire from her job and become a sort of full-time nanny. We could also call on a long list of Becki's friends, many of whom were nurses.

That support sounded very comforting, since I figured I'd need all the help I could get. I wasn't alone in that view. My own mother, when told that I might become a house dad, wrinkled her nose and said, "Keith has no *patience*."

I wasn't so sure she was wrong. I tended to get ticked off when things didn't go my way, and if I had to manage five kids, I figured I could *count* on things not going my way. Plus, I wasn't sure I could handle the workload. What would I do if they all started crying at once? Even worse, I'd never prepared a bottle of formula in my life and I could count on one hand the number of diapers I'd changed.

Truth was, I liked kids, but I didn't particularly like *babies*. Whenever Becki and I were around children, I gravitated toward the ones who were 6 or older—kids you could talk to and do things with. As for the younger ones, let's just say that a few goo-goos went a long way with me.

And yet, a part of me looked forward to it. My dad's job had kept him away a lot when I was a kid, which meant that I didn't really get to know him until a few years ago. I didn't want my kids to have to do that. I wanted them to know me *now*—and this was the perfect way to do it.

Taking care of Becki during the first weeks of her pregnancy gave me time both to learn the ins and outs of housework and to build up my coping skills. In addition to fetching her meals and keeping the house clean, I also took care of Ed and Winston (who was just a puppy and not quite housebroken), plus kept our two aquariums clean. During the worst of our money problems we actually went without things in order to feed the damn fish, mainly because neither of us had the nerve to flush them down the toilet. Becki says that after that incident she knew we'd make good parents. If we'd go to such lengths for a bunch of dime-store fish, imagine what we'd do for our kids. Those fish, by the way, were later wiped out by a fungal infection while Becki was hospitalized. Tragic, but convenient.

Becki says that as the weeks went by and I shouldered more work and responsibility at home, I became ever more patient and tolerant. Whereas in the old days I might get frustrated if, say, the dishwasher acted up, now I simply took a deep breath, counted to 10 and calmed down. Even our families, after watching me tend to both my wife and the house, began to believe that I could handle the babies.

While there were some initial questions about my housekeeping skills, at least there were no doubts about where we would live—at first. We didn't plan to move right away, figuring our two-bedroom house was enough for the kids' first three or four years. We'd keep one bedroom for ourselves, put five cribs in the other and pretty much abandon the rest of the living space to the babies. We would put money away as we went along, then build an addition or buy a new house when the kids got bigger.

It seemed as if we had everything mapped out. That Christmas we purchased our annual commemorative ornament—a pair of ducks, one of which was pregnant, that read, MOM AND DAD TO BE. In spite of our financial troubles, it was a good time. We had each other, we had our health and we had The Plan.

The reality, of course, turned out to be a lot more chaotic. First our financial situation got much worse than we ever imagined, putting us on the edge of bankruptcy. A timely infusion of cash saved our bacon, and for a little while—maybe a week—we kidded ourselves that there would be no more surprises.

Then Becki went into premature labor—a problem partly caused by dehydration from a nasty cold that I brought home from work. Once she stabilized we thought she might get to come home from the hospital, but the doctors thought it too risky to send her back to Bloomington. We were more than an hour from the hospital, meaning that if something went wrong, we might not reach help in time.

That made perfect sense to me. My April 15 drive to the emergency room had shown just how frightening being too far from help can be. We both knew during the drive up that if Becki delivered that day, the babies would almost certainly die. But even worse, all fetuses older than twenty-four weeks are issued death certificates. This meant that we would face not only a terrible immediate tragedy, but five funerals shortly thereafter. We tried not to dwell on this.

Once at the hospital, I had my hands full briefing our families about what was going on. Becki's cramps began to lessen after she was admitted, so I headed home that evening around ten P.M. I wanted to hang around, but Becki was staying on the maternity floor and there was no place for me to sleep. I thought things were looking up, but the next morning I got a call from Becki telling me that she had gone into labor that very evening, while I was seventy miles away, sound asleep. Great. She wasn't too worried at this point, because the crisis had already passed, but I felt enough anxiety for the both of us.

Though I was upset with myself for giving Becki the cold that landed her in the hospital, she considers it a stroke of good luck. She believes that if the cramps from the dehydration hadn't forced her to go to the hospital that day, she would have gone into full labor that night at our house. She would likely have slept right through it, just as she did at the hospital, keeping us from seeking help until a miscarriage was well under way.

That next day I drove up with Becki's parents. Her dad was so overwhelmed by the proceedings that he just sat down in a chair in a corner and clammed up. Her mom, who brought a lifetime supply of new magazines, was also too scared to say much. And Becki, whose brain was scrambled by magnesium sulfate, was about as captivating as a can of creamed corn. Usually I'm the quiet one, but on this day I had to keep the conversation going by explaining where Becki stood medically and what the various tests she was undergoing meant.

Becki and I both had a tough time adjusting during her first week away. She was frightened, unable to sleep and drugged almost to incoherency. I drove up several times, stayed most of the day and then drove back in time for my next evening shift. In addition to the swelling and water retention caused by the drugs, Becki was still fighting off the cold. She took a particular brand of nasal spray for the congestion, and in the middle of that first week she ran out.

One day after work I received a desperate call from my drug-addled wife. "I'm out of nasal spray," she said. "You have to bring me some."

Of course, the particular kind that worked for her was available in every drugstore in the nation, but not at the hospital pharmacy. I had just gotten off my shift and was dog tired after a couple of previous trips to the hospital. "Can't you wait a little while?" I asked. "I'll be up there this weekend."

"I can't wait," Becki sobbed. "I'll be *dead* by this weekend."

I knew this was mostly the magnesium sulfate talking, so I tried to calm her as well as I could over the phone, promising to bring her that weekend all the nasal spray she could ever need. I hung up and prepared to go to bed, but Becki must have been beaming long-distance Guilt Rays at me. Instead of hitting the sack, I got dressed and lead-footed it up to Indianapolis, dragged myself into her hospital room and asked, "What kind of nasal spray do you need?"

Over that first couple of weeks I made several such nasal spray delivery runs. Becki was so groggy that she would misplace bottles, throw them away or not realize she was running low until she took her last dose. Then she'd call and insist she wouldn't live the night without a fresh bottle. Yet when I told her I was on my way she calmed down so much that she was usually asleep by the time I arrived.

Once Becki was in the hospital to stay and I settled into my new bachelor life, I got down to some serious worrying. Given my schedule, there was little else for me to do. Plus, that's my temperament. Becki looks at the bright side and tends to ignore worst-case scenarios, but I can't do that. Ever the pessimist, I examine all the darkest possibilities in loving detail. Expecting the worst has its advantages, however. Whenever the very worst thing *doesn't* happen, I'm usually pleasantly surprised.

Still, in this case I probably worried about fewer things than Becki. Her nursing background was a two-edged sword: It helped her understand what was going on, but it also forced her to think about dozens of syndromes and maladies that I didn't even know existed. While she had a bushel of small things to obsess over, I concentrated on the big issues, such as whether the birth could be delayed long enough, and if Becki could stay healthy.

I found myself hanging around work longer, mainly because I didn't have anything to go home to. My job got particularly rough after weekday trips to the hospital, which usually left me dead tired. On those nights I'd retreat to the back office to do paperwork, then slowly plow through reams of forms while the restaurant ran on autopilot. I never actually nodded off in the walk-in freezer, but I did get groggy. I could still do my job, but everything took about three times as long as usual.

When I got home I'd either call Becki or she'd call me. It depended on who reached for the phone first. We'd talk for hours about nothing. Becki would describe things she saw out her hospital window, or we'd tune to the same channel and watch a TV show together. Sometimes it was almost like we were sitting together in the living room.

We got together almost every single weekend. Becki delighted in showing me how much she'd grown during the week, and I'd usually say something really supportive, like "My God, you have stretch marks on your stretch marks." Becki wasn't vain about them, though she seemed very concerned about whether she had any on her backside. She did, but I always told her she didn't. "No, honey," I'd lie. "Your butt's fine. You only have them where you can see them."

Becki tried to make sure I was there when the nurses checked the babies' heartbeats, because I got such a kick out of listening to them. Since the babies would be premature, our doctors tried to prepare us by providing books on the subject. We also toured the hospital's special-care nursery and looked at some very small premies. They wanted us to know what to expect, so we wouldn't be shocked by how our babies looked.

Well, it *was* a shock, and very frightening for both of us. Instead of being fat, pink, crying babies, the premies we saw had bodies no larger than a hand, arms and legs as thin as pencils, and almost no body fat. They looked more like fetuses than babies. The sight left us slightly overwhelmed, and I wondered again how I could handle such unbelievably fragile-looking creatures. Yet, as

I would learn in the coming months, they don't look as frightening when they're your own.

Sitting in her hospital room was incredibly tedious for Becki, so on weekends I'd push her around the hospital and the grounds in a wheelchair. When the weather improved we started visiting a small patio area behind the building. It was spring, and the air was like a tonic for her after so much time indoors. We also played endless rounds of rummy (which I always won), and I taught Becki numerous variations of solitaire, which I'm told came in handy during the long weekdays.

Deep, meaningful conversations, however, were almost impossible, given the lack of privacy. Occasionally Becki and I tried to discuss finances or some other weighty subject, only to be interrupted by nurses running tests. "Your blood pressure is up, Mrs. Dilley," they'd say. "What's wrong?"

Arguing was totally out of the question. On those rare occasions when we had a disagreement, the babies moved around frantically, which made us think that bickering might be bad for them. Plus, I was outnumbered. If we got the slightest bit snippy with each other, Becki's nurses would flock to her side and look at me like I was Jack the Ripper. Like any normal married couple, we needed to yip at each other occasionally to maintain a healthy relationship. But during our hospital stay, we had to be on our best behavior.

Leaving at the end of each weekend was hard for both of us. Becki would cry and try to stretch out my departure, which meant that I'd sometimes hit the road at one A.M. on Sunday night. I'd head home, crawl in the sack and then get ready for another night on the job. I talked to my coworkers about the pregnancy, but since I wasn't close to anyone there, I'd mostly just share the good things and keep the problems to myself. I wound up keeping *all* the bad stuff to myself, because the person I would normally have vented to—Becki—was too busy living through it to listen to me complain.

Keeping everything bottled up eventually took its toll. Often I'd snap at people at work over trivial issues. Sometimes I spent entire weeks on edge because of things that were happening with Becki.

At the time I had more than just her to worry about. The same summer that Becki became pregnant, my mother was diagnosed with advanced, terminal lung cancer. My mom called to tell me—in such a matter-of-fact manner that I thought she couldn't be *that* sick—that she had cancer and had entered the hospital for tests. We visited her the next day, and when we walked in the room my jaw dropped. Though she sounded strong on the phone, in person she looked terrible: pale and bruised and weighing only 97 pounds. Becki, with her oncology experience, knew instantly that she was terminal—as, I think, did I.

But while most people might have died then and there, mom had something to live for. Over the next several months she went through intense chemical and radiation therapy, eventually winning a mild remission. During Becki's pregnancy she divided her time between her Greenfield home and the hospital she stayed in during treatments.

Often both Becki and Mom were in different hospitals at the same time, Becki for the kids and Mom for chemotherapy. They shared extremely long phone conversations, and once, early on, Mom told Becki she had had a dream. "I dreamed the other day that I saw my grandchildren," she told her. I think that's the reason she lasted as long as she did.

I'd usually visit both of them each weekend, which made for some pretty steep emotional ups and downs. First I would see Becki, then on my way out of town I'd either stop at the hospital or drop by my parents' house. Those trips could be very rough, especially when Mom was in severe pain or feeling down. Hospitals are depressing under the best of circumstances, but they're even worse when someone you love is inside. My mom was never a very emotional person, so the sight of her in tears just tore me up.

In the midst of all these personal issues, our postpregnancy plan also jumped the tracks. In March, Becki's father heard that his job was about to be phased out, and that he would be unemployed by May. After unsuccessfully searching Bloomington for other work, he decided to check out his old childhood haunts, near the tiny northern Indiana burg of Berne.

He quickly landed a job in that distant town, which meant that both he and Becki's mom would have to move *far* away— more than three hours from Bloomington. Becki panicked when she heard the news. She couldn't imagine how we'd manage so many babies without her parents as backup.

Becki's dad quickly hatched a new plan. We would *all* move to the town of Geneva, near Berne, and live together in one big house. Becki and her mom would stay home and tend the babies, while her father and I worked. We would be surrounded by dozens of Berne-area relatives ready, willing and able to help with the kids. On paper it sounded good, particularly in March, when we were still struggling with our finances.

The reality turned out to be a lot more complicated. While Becki was in the hospital, it fell to me to both find a job in the Berne area and to sell our house. I didn't want to put the house on the market until I found work—which didn't happen until

May—and Becki didn't want to open the house for showings while she was still there. When you're as pregnant as she was, there's no way you can dart out on short notice when potential buyers want to stop by. They could have come and looked, as long as they didn't mind having Becki sitting on the couch, watching *them*.

After I landed a job in Berne I finally started showing the house. Only then did I get my first large dose of something that would soon become the centerpiece of my days—housework. Before the pregnancy I had typical male habits: I was a complete slob. But once the house went up for sale, stacking dishes two feet deep on the kitchen counters or allowing dirty clothes to cover the bedroom floor was out of the question. Against my will, I had to become a neat freak.

I particularly hated the laundry—something Becki had handled until the day she went to the hospital. I hated it so much that I let dirty laundry pile up in drifts, which made the day of reckoning that much worse. Actually, I didn't hate washing the clothes as much as I loathed folding them. I would wind up with tons of clean laundry lying around in heaps, waiting to be put away.

As time went by, however, cleaning grew on me. I still didn't like it, but once I got started I washed and scrubbed like a fiend. I was so meticulous that tasks that took Becki an hour would take me three. While I might not get the entire house clean, what I *did* finish was world-class spotless. In Bloomington, mopping the kitchen floor became an elaborate, two-hour process (all for an area not quite as large as a queen-size bed). But vacuuming was—and is—my all-consuming passion. While most people simply run their Hoover through the living room and move on, I first vacuum in one direction, then another, and then *another*, just to make sure that I get every single speck of dust. Becki calls this process Keith Dilley Vacuuming.

Somewhere during my initiation into cleaning, Becki and I went through a rather scary role reversal. Before the pregnancy, she was responsible for cleaning the house and I was responsible for trashing it. But suddenly I found myself using all her favorite lines, including, "Why did you toss those pants on the floor when there's a hamper just two feet away?" I also whined about people dropping things on the clean carpet and not being appreciated for my work.

In early May I landed a food-service job at a small amusement park in the Berne area, near Geneva. I had to start immediately, so I quit my old job and left the keys to our house—where Winston and Ed still lived—with our real estate agent. Then I packed one suitcase and headed for a new life in a strange town. Becki's parents hadn't found a house yet, so I had to stay with Becki's grandparents.

Since I was stuck more than three hours away, the care and feeding of Winston and Ed fell to our agent, who needless to say went above and beyond the call of duty in helping us. Ed was a very grumpy cat, but a few weeks of living on his own and seeing how bad life could *really* be turned him around. Suddenly he became the most lovable animal on earth.

Becki, for her part, had always considered the big orange cat to be the sum of feline perfection. Over the years she'd developed an extremely close relationship with him that can only be described as, well, *sick*. I mean, if Ed and I were on a sinking ship and Becki could save just one of us, I'm not 100 percent sure whom she'd pick. This made The Ed Incident all the more terrible.

One night while I was staying at her grandparents' house, I received a frantic call from Becki. The real estate agent couldn't find Ed and thought he might have run away. Becki freaked out when she heard the news, becoming so upset that her doctors

Ed, our "first child"

feared she might go into labor. She briefly contemplated going to Bloomington to look for the cat herself, until she thought of a better idea: Send me. Even though I lived almost a half day's drive from our old house, Becki called to ask if I could please, please, please immediately drive to Bloomington to search for Ed.

I didn't go. I'd do anything for Becki, but the cat was on his own. We needn't have worried. It seems that Ed retreated into the crawl space under the house through a hole in our garage whenever the real estate agent stopped by. When several days passed without her seeing him, she figured he'd run away. Only after she came in unexpectedly and spied him lounging in the living room did she understand what had happened.

The mystery was solved in a day, but it left me with an uneasy feeling. I was so far away that there was nothing I could do. Talk about feeling helpless. At least when I was in Bloomington I could get to the hospital in an hour if need be. In Geneva I was trapped.

But as I soon discovered, it *was* possible to get to the hospital in an hour from Geneva—if you have the right motivation. Only two weeks after moving, Becki called and told me that she was having the babies that afternoon. I jumped in my Chevy Cavalier, slammed the pedal to the floor and flew down the country roads so fast that the needle on my speedometer, which only went up to 85, spun off the dial. I pulled into the parking lot just a shade over an hour later. This was one birthday I wasn't going to miss.

❀ 6 ❀

HAPPY BIRTH DAZE

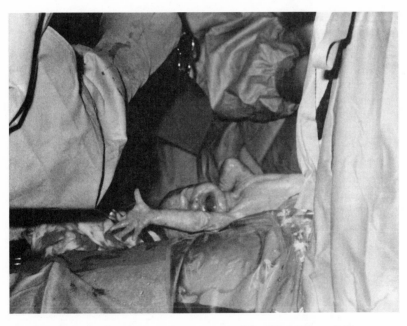

Adrian makes his dramatic entrance on May 25, 1993, at 5:31 P.M.

❀ ❀ ❀ ❀ ❀ ❀

BECKI

The day the kids were born felt like the opening night of a Broadway show. We'd rehearsed endlessly for the big production, and now it was time to perform. But no one expected our surprise guest star—an undetected sixth baby who nearly brought the house down.

I didn't immediately realize that May 25 was the big day. That morning I was more concerned with why the right side of my face suddenly stopped working. When I looked in the bathroom mirror, I briefly wondered if I had finally suffered the stroke my doctors feared. It certainly *looked* like one.

But my nursing experience told me otherwise. Unlike that of a typical stroke victim, my thinking was clear and I had complete control over the rest of my body. Whatever had happened seemed confined to my face.

I stepped out of the bathroom and called for a nurse, who in turn called a neurologist. After giving me a handful of tests, including having me stand on one leg to check my balance, she concluded that I suffered from Bell's palsy, a fairly common form of paralysis among pregnant women. Water retention and the sheer mass of the babies had pinched off a facial nerve, causing temporary loss of motor control.

That explanation—along with the assurance that Bell's palsy was neither particularly dangerous nor usually permanent—greatly eased my fears. For the rest of that morning I went about my business more or less as usual. The pinched nerve affected my face, but the rest of me felt fine. When my mom and sister visited later that morning I told them the paralysis was only a mild setback, and certainly nothing to worry about.

I was given a taco salad for lunch, which wasn't the best choice for someone with poor facial control. For every bite that reached my mouth, another landed in my lap. My sister and mom, far from being overly concerned, laughed with me while I struggled to eat.

In the midst of my meal, Dr. Smirz stopped by, looked me over and announced that the next day I would begin a new round of steroids to control the palsy. And then, in a quiet, measured voice, she added, "Becki, we need to start you on steroids right away, so at about five o'clock we're going to go ahead and do the C-section. You're body's had just about enough of being pregnant. Let's go ahead. The babies are ready."

I nearly dropped my fork. Everyone was so sanguine about the palsy that I didn't consider it a very big deal. And it usually isn't when it's treated promptly. But I couldn't take the steroids while I was pregnant, which meant it was time for me *not* to be pregnant. The countdown had begun.

Before I could say anything, my mom and sister screamed with joy, hugged each other and jumped up and down. Dr. Smirz, who was obviously very nervous herself, looked at them as if they were out of their minds. The last thing she said as she walked out of the room, more to herself than to me, was "I've got lots to do."

She did indeed—and only about five hours in which to do it. I, too, had plenty of things to take care of. My sister immediately drove back to Bloomington to pick up my younger brother, while Mom stayed to help call friends and relatives.

That was the plan, anyway. Mom was okay for a little while, but as the enormity of events sank in, she quickly lost control. First, she couldn't use the phone. Again and again she'd try to dial an outside line, attempt to punch in the calling card number, then mutter, "What do I do?" and hang up in frustration. If being a basket case was a medical disorder, Mom would have been in intensive care. She was so frightened she shook.

After a few minutes of this, I took over the phoning duties. The first people I reached were Keith and my dad, who both worked at the same Berne amusement park. Dad was dumb-founded when he heard, as was Keith. "You've still got plenty of time," I told Keith in my best fake-calm voice. "Go home and take a quick shower, change your clothes and come on down. Drive carefully." Keith lit out for Indianapolis immediately, while my dad, who couldn't walk away from his job on such short notice, stayed to finish his shift. But he, too, made it to the hospital just before the delivery.

I mentioned the Bell's palsy to Keith so my appearance wouldn't surprise him. Actually, *I* was becoming slightly freaked out by the way I looked. The paralysis gradually worsened as the hours passed. My speech became more slurred, my facial muscles went completely slack and I couldn't close my right eye. But I had so much work to do that I couldn't dwell on my condition, or the C-section, either—a blessing, really. In addition to making phone calls and keeping an eye on Mom, I also read and signed reams of consent forms—all carefully stacked in five piles, one for each baby—covering almost every medical procedure known to man.

Those projects kept me from worrying, but they couldn't keep my mind off the passing minutes. Mom took care of that. She kept saying, "Four hours and eighteen minutes until I'm a grandma," "Four hours and five minutes until I'm a grandma," etc. That is, when she was actually in the room. She was so nervous that she kept darting down to the front entrance to get some air, or else patrolled the halls aimlessly, trying to walk off the stress.

Other times she sat in a rocking chair in the corner of my room, making busy-talk to any doctor or nurse within earshot. Every few minutes she'd get a cup of coffee or a soft drink, take one sip and then set it on the window ledge by her chair. Then, a few minutes later she'd tell me in a perky but brittle-sounding voice, "I'm going to go get a Coke," or "I'm going to get something to eat. Can I get you something from the gift shop?" Then she'd excuse herself and go get *another* drink. By the time they wheeled me down to the operating room, the shelf next to her chair held an entire row of barely touched pop cans and coffee cups.

As the big event drew nearer, I was transferred to a labor and delivery room near the two surgical suites set aside for me. My room slowly filled with doctors, technicians and nurses, all of them scrambling to complete various preparations. Keith arrived at around three-thirty, looking extremely nervous. Thank God he got there when he did, because I was just about to receive an epidural anesthetic. The epidural would numb me from the waist down but leave me awake and alert so I could see the birth. Unfortunately epidurals must be administered at the base of the spine, with a very large needle.

Having just finished signing all the consent forms, I decided to go to the bathroom before receiving the anesthetic. I was on an IV at the time, so I asked Keith to hold up the bag. Unfortunately Keith, who normally is such an understanding guy, happened to say exactly the wrong thing at precisely the wrong moment. I was enormously, fantastically pregnant, suffering from Bell's palsy and preparing to go under the knife, and Keith had the exquisitely poor judgment to mention that holding up the IV bag hurt his arm.

His *arm* hurt? I poured all of the morning's fear and stress into a two-minute tirade, then dissolved into tears. Poor Keith. I was more frightened than I realized. I needed to take it out on someone, and he was it. By the time I got back to my bed we were both fine, but I was through being a trouper. From that point on I wanted to be the patient and have people look after *me*. Keith would have to handle everything else.

He soon had plenty to contend with. The epidural turned out to be a very messy affair. The anesthesiologist who administered it had me lean over a table while Keith held my hands. I squeezed the Dickens out of them. I was on blood thinner and had developed an enormous number of extra blood vessels to support the pregnancy, so with each poke of the needle I bled profusely. It took five attempts to place the nerve block properly, leaving me covered with blood. I kept encouraging the doctor to try again, because I didn't want to use a general anesthetic, which would cause me to sleep through the delivery.

After the epidural it was time for the main event. As the clock ticked down to 5:00 P.M. everyone hustled to take care of last-minute details. In the midst of this controlled chaos, my mom, for the final time, wandered back into the room after pacing around outdoors. "I was talking to the landscaper," she told anyone who would listen. "He was telling me about numerology. He believes it's possible to foretell the future by examining important combinations of numbers . . ."

And so on. Eventually a nurse pulled me aside and asked if Mom needed a Valium. I thought she was joking, but she didn't crack a smile. "I'm serious," she said. "Do you think she needs something to cope?" Eventually, one of the two nurses assigned to look after me began looking after my mom instead.

At 5:00 P.M. they tried to transfer me onto a gurney, only to discover that my bed couldn't be raised high enough to roll me from one to the other. So instead they wheeled the entire bed down the hall to the operating room, where a group of nurses lifted me onto the operating table. Imagine that—a bunch of nurses accomplishing something that once required six burly firemen.

Considering how many people either helped with or attended the birth, I'm amazed anyone was left at the hospital's front desk to answer the phones. The medical teams filled two operating rooms. In the first, Dr. Smirz, Dr. McLaughlin, two anesthesiologists and two scrub nurses prepared to deliver the babies. Another nurse and a doctor observed, and three more "circulating nurses" waited to help out as needed. In addition, two three-person neonatal teams stood by. Each consisted of an intensive-care nurse, neonatologist or pediatrician and respiratory therapist, and each team had its own infant warmer. The other, "overflow," operating room contained three more neonatal teams, each of which was to devote itself to a particular baby.

Even with two operating rooms, conditions were still crowded—and they got worse when I was wheeled in. But all those people were necessary, because anything could happen during the delivery. Dr. Smirz worried that I might suffer a hemorrhage or an embolism, so she tried to plan for every contingency.

Four units of blood were prepped for immediate use, along with everything necessary for an emergency hysterectomy. Drug "cocktails" for almost every possible ailment were drawn up in advance and taped to the walls of the operating room. Each packet included a syringe and a name tag, so the nurses could rip them off the walls and use them instantly.

This was serious stuff, and everyone involved knew it. I could easily have died from any number of pre- or postnatal complications, and no one knew in what condition the babies would arrive. Yet as the big moment approached, the team members laughed and joked as if the delivery was a sure thing. Having a medical background myself, I didn't find this strange. Preparing for a major procedure is like getting ready for an athletic event. You have to get psyched, go in with a positive attitude and believe you'll succeed.

There was no shortage of people who thought themselves equal to the challenge. There was even a small battle over who got to witness the birth. At first Dr. Smirz said that only those directly involved in the delivery would be admitted. Eventually, however, the guest list grew to include a handful of interested doctors, many of the nurses who had attended me during my hospital stay, the hospital PR rep and a staffer with a video camera, who filmed the birth. No doubt about it, this was a very hot ticket. Little did we know how useful all those spare people would soon become.

Once we settled into the OR, Keith planted himself on a stool near the top of the operating table, beside my head. My right arm was stretched out to accommodate a blood pressure cuff and an IV, and Keith held on to my left hand. As Dr. Smirz prepared to make the incision for the caesarean, the teams in the next operating room started singing "Happy Birthday."

The anesthesiologist adjusted an overhead mirror so I could watch. The only thing that worried me at this point was that I wasn't 100 percent sure the anesthetic had worked. "Keith," I whispered, "I don't think I'm numb." But Keith, who was watching the doctors remove my cerclage scar and begin the C-section incision, reassured me that I was.

I had no feeling from the chest down, which gave me an odd sense of detachment during the procedure. It was like watching a medical show on TV. When Dr. Smirz reached inside me and pulled out the babies, it felt as if someone was sitting on my chest. There was no pain—just some very strange sensations.

During the pregnancy Keith developed the habit of patting my head or shoulder during exams and tests, and this day was no different. But this time he was so nervous that he literally beat me around the head and neck, causing me to jiggle on the table. Dr. Smirz, who was in the midst of operating, shot him a quick look, and someone tactfully suggested that he just hold my hand. I hung on to it very tightly, so that he couldn't move around anymore.

The C-section itself was so fast and businesslike that delivering the babies took only about five minutes. The first baby, Brenna Rose, made the most dramatic entrance. I remember looking up at the mirror and seeing this blue, hand-size object crying a fitful "Wah, wah, wah." Keith and I clutched each other's hands and I started to cry. Then came Julian Emerson, so fast on the heels of Brenna that it shocked me. Dr. Smirz would pull out a baby, hand him or her off and immediately go to the next child. The deliveries were only about 30 seconds apart.

In the next few moments Quinn Everett and Claire Diane were born and instantly given to the teams responsible for them.

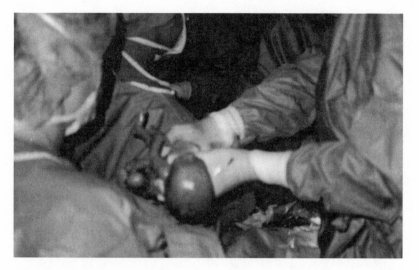

Our first child, Brenna, just as we heard her first cry, on May 25, 1993, at 5:28 P.M.

The team members wrapped the kids in blankets and took them to their assigned areas, where they were examined to make sure their airways were clear, cleaned up, placed in infant warmers, put on oxygen and connected to heart monitors.

At the beginning of the delivery, the only audible heartbeat was mine, which registered as a steady beep-beep from the electrocardiograph connected to me. But as the babies were born and placed on EKGs, I heard first one new pinging sound, then another and another, until the room was filled with gentle electronic beeping. Suddenly there were heartbeats all over the place.

I will remember the arrival of Ian Michael—the last of the five "expected" babies—for the rest of my life. He looked like a frog boy, because when they brought him out his little legs were kicking furiously. He does that to this day whenever I pick him up. "That's a live one," I thought as they bundled him off to his warmer.

After Ian's delivery, the tension level began dropping and clean-up operations commenced. Throughout the delivery I focused completely on the babies and forgot about everything else. But once I thought it was over, I looked around the room and noticed all the extra equipment on hand for emergencies. For the first time I felt a major case of the creeps.

Moments later I received a drug to relax me, along with something else to help my uterus contract and expel the placentas. Dr. Smirz was doing a last internal check to make sure everything was all right, when her hand touched something totally unexpected—a foot.

She didn't share this news with the outside world right away, however. It took a good ten seconds for the implications to sink in. A sixth baby. Sextuplets.

"Oh boy," I recall her saying.

All activity in the OR ceased for several seconds.

"We have a sixth baby here," she said.

"That's not funny, Lynda," said the neonatologist.

But Dr. Smirz had proof positive. She extracted the sixth baby, soon to be named Adrian Reed, and said, "Surprise! We've got him. Where do you want him?"

The entire operating room exploded into activity. All the nurses invited to watch the procedure suddenly vanished out the door. Everyone scrambled to round up more equipment and support personnel, and the person videotaping the births—who had turned off his camera after Ian was born and thus missed the chaos—was almost knocked flat. The head of the hospital's PR department just stood in a corner chanting "Oh no, oh no."

Dr. Smirz feared that the last baby, because we had ignored him for so long, might be stillborn. She needn't have worried. Adrian, who entered the world at 5:31 P.M., was the biggest and hardiest of the lot, weighing in at a hefty 2 pounds, 13 ounces and crying lustily. The stealth baby was revealed to the world at last. Lacking his own infant warmer, he was placed in the same one as Brenna.

At that point Keith was ready for anything. "Is there a seventh baby?" he asked the doctors.

"I don't *see* a seventh," said Dr. Smirz, herself almost giddy from the surprise. Suddenly the enormity of what had happened dawned on everyone. Quintuplets was a big deal, but sextuplets was national news. The OR got louder and louder as excited conversations began. As for me, I think the stress of the moment took its toll. I looked up at the smiling face of my anesthesiologist and said, "I can't breathe. I'm going to barf."

Then the sedative hit me, putting me in a fog for the rest of the day. I was wheeled out of the OR, back to the labor and delivery room and then to the intensive-care unit, where I spent the next two days. As I was wheeled away and the babies headed for the special-care nursery, Keith walked down to the waiting room to brief our families. Keith isn't a great public speaker under the best circumstances, but on this occasion words failed him entirely. Unable to speak, he just poked his head in the waiting room, smiled and held up six fingers. I couldn't have said it better myself.

❋ 7 ❋

MEET THE PRESS

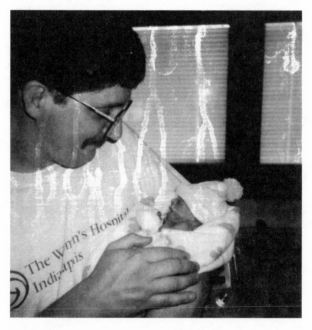

Keith holds Quinn for the first time, three days after the babies' birth.

KEITH

After the birth, Becki was numbed by painkillers. I was just plain numb. I walked out of the operating room in a happy, dazed cloud, shuffling alongside Becki's bed as she was wheeled to her recovery room. Though I was glad for my wife and concerned for the kids, the enormity of what had happened hadn't struck me yet. But it would. Would it ever. I didn't realize it at the time, but the next week would be my first taste of what fathering sextuplets was really like.

But first there was time for some fun. As soon as I found a phone, I called my mom, who was too sick to come to the hospital. "Mom, the babies are here," I said. "There are four boys and two girls." It took a second for her to do the math, but when she had she was thrilled. I liked her reaction so much that I pulled the same stunt on everyone else I called.

Not that I had to contact all that many people. The media took care of our birth announcements. The hospital wanted to keep everything secret until the next morning, to give Becki and the kids time to stabilize. Fat chance. Word of the sextuplets leaked to a local radio station before we made it out of the OR. Soon the hospital parking lot filled with TV news vans and the lobby overflowed with reporters. Everyone, it seemed, wanted the scoop on the babies.

At first I was just as curious and uninformed as everyone else. During that first evening I visited the special-care nursery, but I couldn't see much of the kids. Mostly I just stared at the backs of the people who surrounded their isolettes, caring for them. My dad and I sat on chairs outside the nursery, watching medical personnel run in and out—not the most comforting sight for a new father. We were told that the kids were in as good a condition as could be expected, but little else.

By nightfall the stress of the day had taken its toll on me. Since I couldn't stay with Becki in her recovery room, I decided to spend the night at my brother's house in nearby Greenfield. That evening the hospital, to quiet the rising demand for information about the babies, held a packed press conference to update the local media. Many of the doctors who had attended the birth were there, but it was announced that the still-anonymous parents were in seclusion and unavailable for interviews. I know this because I was "secluded" in the back of the room, unrecognized, during the press conference.

My brother and I eased out of the meeting at around nine-thirty and bolted for the lobby, where we ran a gauntlet of reporters who quizzed us as we passed.

"You guys know who the father is?" one asked.

"Father of what?" we said. "What are you guys talking about?"

It wasn't until the next morning that I fully understood just what Becki and I were in for. I woke up early and switched on

CNN, where, to my amazement, I heard a story about a set of recently born sextuplets. I did a double take. *Another* set? I must have still been groggy, because it took a few moments for me to figure out that they were talking about *us*.

When I returned to the hospital, the craziness began in earnest—and I realized just how unprepared I was. I had the entire week off from my job, and planned to spend almost every waking moment at the hospital. But I had dashed out of Geneva with only the clothes on my back. I became very familiar with my rugby shirt and blue jeans, because I kept them on for the next three days.

Becki and I quickly settled into a routine. Each morning we'd go see the kids, then spend the rest of the day coping with the blizzard of forms and reports associated with the babies—everything from birth certificates to applications for Social Security numbers. That's the real reason so few people have sextuplets: They can't handle the paperwork. At night I slept on a foldout bed in Becki's room. I use the term "sleep" loosely, because neither of us got much rest that first week. Becki was constantly awakened for late-night tests, and my foldout bed was about as comfortable as, well, a foldout bed.

Every time we turned around, there was another knock on the door—and not all of them were welcome. After news of the birth broke nationwide, it seemed like every grocery-store tabloid and TV talk show in the world tried to contact us. Apparently they thought that six newborns would fit right in with Sunday School Teachers Who Kill and Men Who Cheat on Their Mistresses. Maury Povich sent us stuffed animals, and one tabloid dispatched a reporter to roam the hospital corridors looking for me. The medical staff helped me stay a step ahead by warning me whenever he approached.

Soon I was being paged more often than the doctors. In retrospect, I suppose we could have ignored the requests. At the time, however, it was all so new, and Becki and I were both so shell-shocked, that this never occurred to us. It wouldn't have been *polite*.

Finally the hospital took the situation in hand. A security guard was placed outside Becki's door to ward off close encounters of the media kind, and we created a code that friends and relatives could use to phone us. Everyone else would have to leave a message. From then on, the only people who rang our room were the ones who told the operator they wanted to speak to "Ed Winston."

It worked—sort of. Inside the hospital we were reasonably safe, but I still drew stares when I ventured into the great outdoors. I made plenty of field trips, both to see my mom and to get food for Becki. She was finally off her dreaded no-salt diet and eager to sample normal fare. At least I didn't have to sneak in the sweet-and-sour pork under my coat anymore. On top of everything else, we were closing on our Bloomington house. Amid all my other worries, I also had to fax offers and counteroffers to our real estate agent.

Two days after the birth, the hospital arranged a small press gathering for Becki and me—just a couple of print reporters and a pool cameraman, we were told. Figuring that an interview might blunt some of the media interest, we readily consented. First, however, I took care of some personal business. There was no way I could meet the press wearing my now-fragrant rugby shirt, so I slipped out to a local department store to get another outfit. We had almost no cash, so I bought the cheapest possible thing—a pair of discount blue jeans and a pack of three black T-shirts. I looked like a hood, but so what? It was just a couple of reporters.

Wrong. We realized just how badly we'd misjudged the situation when cameramen met us as we stepped off the elevator, then followed us all the way to the designated meeting room, which was packed with reporters. Of all the people in America, I think Becki and I were the least prepared to meet the press. Becki was in a wheelchair with half her face still paralyzed by Bell's palsy, and I was so intimidated by the crowd that all I could manage were one-syllable answers.

Thankfully, Becki rose to the occasion, handling the bulk of the questions while I smiled and tried to fade into the wallpaper. We called it the "wonderful" press conference, because she used that word roughly twice in every sentence. When the meeting ended, the cameramen followed us out into the hall and back to the elevators. No doubt about it—this thing was big.

In spite of all the distractions, our thoughts centered on the babies. During that first week, the medical staff tried to familiarize us with the kids, even though we could rarely get close to them. Our most intimate contact was usually touching their feet. The nurses also took snapshots of the kids for us to keep in Becki's room.

During that first week I developed some practical concerns. While Becki was pregnant, caring for so many babies had been an abstract problem. Now, however, it was very, very real. I thought about it constantly, wondering how we'd find the money and time to manage so many. And I wondered how we—but mostly I—would adapt to this new lifestyle.

Diapers frightened me the most. At the time I hadn't changed many, and didn't plan on changing many more. In the early days of the pregnancy—before I learned the true state of affairs—I figured that if we had only one kid I would have to change perhaps two diapers a day, or fourteen a week, tops. No problem. I could

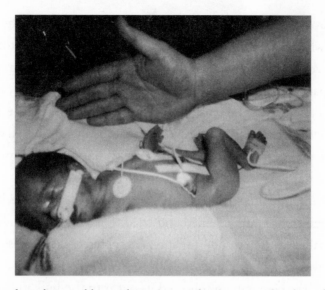

Brenna, three hours old, weighing 2 pounds, 6 ounces. Keith took this photo and brought it to Becki, who was in the recovery room. This was her first good look at her baby.

deal with that. With sextuplets, however, that comforting scenario went out the window.

I decided I wouldn't think about it until the big moment arrived. Little did I realize that it would come so soon after the birth. One day while Becki and I were visiting the nursery, a nurse suddenly asked me if I would like to change one of the babies.

"Yes he would," said Becki, before I could respond.

It was showtime. The nurse opened up the side panel of one of the isolettes and I leaned over and ducked inside. These days I can change all six kids in five minutes blindfolded, but that first time was nightmarish. I spent ten minutes with my head wedged in the isolette, sweating, nervous and all thumbs.

Removing the diaper was easy, I discovered, but cleaning the baby and fastening on a new diaper was murder. It didn't help that the babies were only slightly larger than my hand. They were so dainty that I feared I might hurt them. When I finally finished, I wondered how I would ever manage the kids if changing a single diaper took so long. I didn't realize that practice—*lots* of practice—makes perfect.

But that practice would have to wait. On the Tuesday after Memorial Day, I was forced to return to Geneva to my job. I'd burned all my vacation time, which meant that from then on I could see my wife and kids only on weekends. I kept up on events mostly through daily progress reports that Becki gave me over the phone. It wasn't much, but under the circumstances it would have to do. As it turned out, Becki would have plenty to report over the coming weeks.

❀ 8 ❀

LEARNING PROCESS

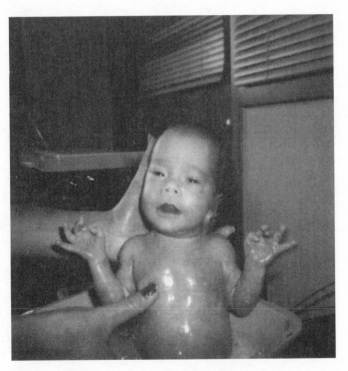

Nurse Julie gives Brenna her first bath.

BECKI

Almost a year after the birth of the sextuplets, Keith and I organized the press clippings, photos and videotapes from the babies' first days into a scrapbook. We thought it would be fun, but watching the tapes proved more unsettling than entertaining.

I don't think we realized until then just how fragile and vulnerable our kids were. The babies spent most of their first three months in the hospital, lying in individual plastic isolettes. They were surrounded by clicking, humming machines and connected to oxygen lines, IVs, feeding tubes and monitors. When I saw this on video, all the fear and uncertainty I'd felt at that time came rushing back. I sat in front of the TV and cried.

On one tape Keith looked at Brenna and said, "She's looking a lot better. I think we're through the worst of it." That was especially poignant, since I knew that one of Brenna's lungs collapsed shortly after that video was made.

Those first days seem far more frightening in hindsight than they did at the time. Keith and I both knew that the babies faced

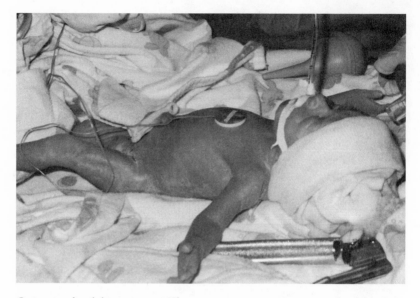

Quinn in the delivery room. The equipment was monitoring his heartbeat and helping him breathe. It may look overwhelming, but actually he was doing very well for a prematurely born child.

a long hospital stay while their lungs developed and they put on weight, but we were too excited about finally becoming parents to dwell endlessly on potential problems.

We got the kids' vital statistics on the evening of the C-section. Baby A, Brenna Rose, weighed 2 pounds, 6 ounces; Baby B, Julian Emerson, weighed 2 pounds, 13 ounces; Baby C, Quinn Everett, weighed 2 pounds, 2 ounces; Baby D, Claire Diane, weighed 2 pounds, 7 ounces; Baby E, Ian Michael, weighed 2 pounds, 11 ounces; and Baby F, Adrian Reed, weighed 2 pounds, 13 ounces. We named them on the spot, sight-unseen, using all four of our boy names and the first two from our girls' list (Anna Lynn and Kay Leigh didn't make the cut).

All the kids passed their first night in critical but stable condition. None faced any special difficulties save for Claire. She had a bowel movement while still in utero, potentially making her vulnerable to infection—a possibility that never materialized. Barring medical complications, the babies, who were nine weeks premature, needed to gain weight and learn to breathe on their own, without ventilators or pure oxygen, before they could go home. Until then, they would stay in the hospital.

The day after the birth I was formally introduced to my children—though it wasn't easy. I wanted to see the babies as soon as I awoke that morning, but every time Keith and I got ready to go, he'd be called away to do a TV or newspaper interview about the births (it never occurred to us that we didn't have to respond). As the hours passed and everyone from my mom to the nurses took turns visiting the kids, I grew more and more frustrated. Finally at around four-thirty P.M. I burst into tears and asked if someone, anyone, would please take me to see my babies. My evening-shift nurse, incensed by the delay, refused to allow any more interviews until I got my wish.

That did the trick. I piled into a wheelchair and Keith pushed me to the nursery, where I went from isolette to isolette, looking at and touching each baby. I remember the nurses coming over and saying, "Mrs. Dilley, I'm taking care of Julian," or "I'm taking care of Adrian," explaining what they were doing and then opening the access panels to the isolettes and letting me touch the babies' feet. I can't remember which one I saw first, mainly because I was crying too hard to tell. Even Keith, Mr. Stone Face, cried, and my nurse wept so hard she had to have a tissue.

It was utterly overwhelming. For the very first time I faced a problem that I'll deal with for the rest of my life—how to divide my time fairly among six children. I wanted to stare at each baby endlessly, yet I knew I had to move on if I wanted to see them all.

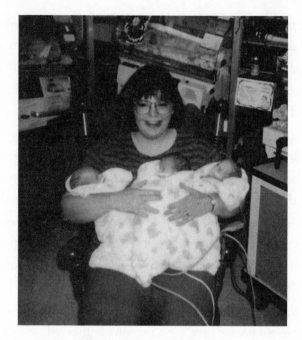

Becki visiting one-month-olds Quinn, Claire and Adrian in the hospital. The nurses wanted to see how many children Becki could hold at once.

The babies stayed on ventilators for their first couple of nights, then were slowly weaned off the machines and allowed to breathe on their own, with supplemental oxygen. On the third day after the birth part of Brenna's lung collapsed, but even then no one panicked—except, for a little while, Keith and me. It could have been a life-threatening problem, but she was surrounded by so many physicians and so much technology that the danger was slight. After constant care, the lung reinflated within a couple of days.

During those early days I seemed to have more physical diffi-culties than the kids. My C-section scar wouldn't stop bleeding, and when the sutures were removed just before I was to be dis-charged, the wound opened again.

This was both frightening and uncomfortable, but I managed to talk the doctors into letting me leave anyway. Normally hospitals don't release people with open, six-inch wounds, but because I was a nurse and knew how to keep it cleaned and dressed, they let me go. The incision could be sutured shut again after the tissue had a chance to heal on its own.

I felt decidedly mixed emotions when I checked out of the hospital with Keith that day, only eight days after the birth. I was anxious to be free, but I felt strange about leaving the babies for the first time. I also left behind my built-in support group, the nurses who had tended me for weeks. It was like saying goodbye to a surrogate family.

The problem with my C-section scar probably saved me from a tearful round of goodbyes. None of my nurses thought I would be discharged on schedule, so they didn't make a fuss about my "last day." I understand there were some astonished people at the hospital the next day when they signed in and found me gone. Maybe it was for the best, because I'm not very good at farewells. I cried when we left the hospital, and I *kept* crying while we stood in line at a nearby drugstore, waiting to have some prescriptions filled.

But I wasn't going far. I planned to stay at a nearby apartment complex that had donated a furnished flat for however long the babies were hospitalized. After my discharge we first ate a celebration dinner at a nearby Mexican restaurant, then visited a grocery store to stock up on supplies. After so many weeks of bed rest and hospitalization, it felt wonderful to step outside, breathe fresh air and go wherever I wanted. But sitting around for so long had taken its toll, as I discovered at the grocery store when I became winded while walking down the aisles.

Next we visited the donated apartment. Keith had already dropped off several boxes full of my clothes and personal items, but I was still nervous about the arrangement. Ever the small-town girl, I feared staying in Indianapolis by myself. Keith, who had to go back to Geneva that night for his job, advised me to keep the windows closed at all times to ward off the roving gangs of machine gun–toting criminals we assumed infested the city.

Keith went to Berne as soon as I settled in, and a feeling of terrible loneliness came over me as soon as he drove away. For the last few weeks I had been able to get help just by pushing a button, but now I was totally on my own. I didn't even have a car, since the C-section incision kept me from driving.

Actually, I wasn't *totally* alone. When I first opened the apartment door I'd been greeted by our cat, Ed, whom Keith had brought up from Bloomington to stay with me. We hadn't seen each other for so long that he hissed at me, the little jerk. But later that night he jumped up on my bed and fell asleep on my stomach, just as he used to. And so I passed my first, restless night in yet another home away from home. For someone with such a big family, I pondered, I seemed to spend an awful lot of time by myself.

Over the next two weeks I developed a daily routine. Every morning I got up, watched CNN and sat by the phone, waiting for my nine A.M. progress report on the babies. I didn't shower until after the call because I was petrified that I wouldn't reach the phone in time if it rang. I took down all the information, so that I could recite it to Keith when I phoned him in the evening.

Afterward I'd shower, dress, take a cab to the hospital and spend the rest of the day with the babies. Those cab rides got to be expensive, however—especially since we didn't have much discretionary income. A couple of times I couldn't make it to the hospital because I didn't have the seven-dollar one-way fare.

Sometimes I'd call a cab in the morning, then catch a ride with one of the nurses that evening.

Once at the hospital I'd go from isolette to isolette, looking at each baby while the nurses told me about their progress. Instead of an in-depth medical analysis, they offered a more personal view of the children—the kind of news that parents eat up. Quinn, I was told, would be my best-behaved baby, because he was so easygoing. Julian, I learned, had a terrible temper, and Claire seemed very demanding.

I tried breast-feeding, but I couldn't produce enough milk to support all those appetites. I was able to pump a little bit (all of it went to Julian, the weakest), but after about six weeks my body gave up. I was simply too physically drained to produce enough.

Each of the nurses seemed to bond with particular babies. Julian had two caretakers who knew him much better than I did, and Quinn's respiratory therapist said she was going to marry him when he grew up. I loved to hear such comments, because I knew the nurses saw the babies as more than just tiny patients in plastic boxes.

I spent hours in the nursery talking with the staff about what the babies were like and what sorts of adults they'd become. "Adrian's so sweet and lovable, he's going to be your loving one," they'd say, or "Quinn's going to be a lady-killer." Soon those nurses became friends. We talked not just about the children, but about what they'd done on dates, how Keith and I were doing, and the conversational lifeblood of all nurses—gossip, gossip, gossip.

Looking back, it was a fun, relaxing time. I felt so laid-back because, by and large, the babies made steady, rapid progress.

But not everyone did equally well. On June 3 I was told that Julian wasn't breathing well on his own, and might have to be

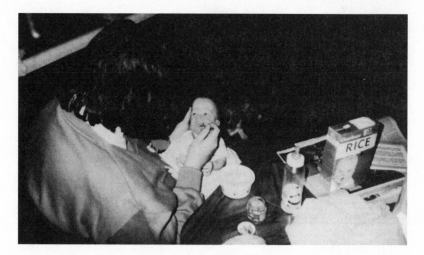

Becki feeds Quinn his first bowl of cereal. Winston, our Welsh corgi, is in the background. Unfortunately, Winston had to be sent away to another family shortly after the children came home. The dog couldn't handle all of the attention from the babies.

placed back on a ventilator. This was very bad news, since getting him to breathe on his own was the first step to ending his reliance on pure oxygen. Since prolonged exposure can cause lung damage and blindness in premies, each day he stayed on oxygen increased the chances of long-term complications.

Worrying about Julian soon became a habit. During my nine A.M. phone reports it seemed they always saved him for last, and I never breathed a sigh of relief until I heard how he was doing. The story was always the same: He labored furiously to breathe, taking as many as eighty breaths per minute, and though he managed to stay off the respirator he couldn't survive without pure oxygen. That report always set me on edge. I never allowed myself to wonder if Julian might die, but I did worry that he would suffer some long-term disability.

It was sad to watch him laboring in his isolette. He was such an unhappy baby. His face scrunched up and it seemed as if he needed every muscle in his body just to draw breath. He was also very irritable and would fight to get away from the oxygen. If the nurses ran a tube down his nose, he'd try to pull it out; and if they put his head in an oxygen tent, he struggled to escape. Finally they simply pumped the entire isolette full of oxygen.

Julian couldn't take formula from a bottle, and handling disturbed him so much that I held him only once during his entire hospital stay. In fact, I rarely touched him at all. He became very, very withdrawn. Locked in a painful struggle for every breath, he loathed human contact. I began seeing Julian as "the sick one," and I wondered if it might always be so.

But while Julian struggled, the other babies thrived. All of them craved ever more attention as they grew stronger, especially Claire. When I toured the isolettes in the morning, she would cry as soon as I passed her by. She seemed content so long as the nurses and I hovered over her, but she fussed as soon as she stopped receiving so much attention. The nurses would always say, "Claire, you had your turn," when she cried.

Quinn, or Quinny, as we called him, was all over his isolette. His favorite game was to take off his diaper and paint the walls with its contents. Each baby had a tiny stuffed toy in his or her isolette, and Quinn's bear was regularly turned over to me for cleaning. "You might want to wash this," the nurses would say grimly as they handed it over. I still have those toys, but Quinn's is in terrible condition thanks to all those voyages through the spin cycle.

On weekends I made the rounds with Keith, who drove down on Friday evenings. The babies grew so rapidly that to him they seemed to double in size each week. We spent almost every waking moment of each weekend with the children. The nurses allowed me to hold the babies and change their diapers, but when Keith was around I let him take over. *Sometimes*. It's hard to believe now, but in those days we actually argued over who got to change diapers. "Please let me change them," Keith would say. "You get to do it all week long."

Occasionally we'd go out to dinner, though never to fast-food places. The nurses suggested that we visit sit-down restaurants, since we probably wouldn't see the inside of one again after the kids came home. They were so-o-o right. Looking back, I wish we had relished those last days of freedom more. At the time, however, all we could think about was how great it would be when our kids came home. I guess you always want what you don't have.

About ten days after I left the hospital, the doctors sutured my C-section incision closed again. This time it healed normally, clearing me to drive. On weekends Keith still came down to see the babies, but on Sunday we'd drive to Geneva, where my parents had purchased a house.

Keith would spend each Sunday night trying to convince me to be there when he got home from work on Monday evening. Just as I had once begged him to spend an extra night when he visited me in the hospital, now he asked me again and again to stay one or two extra days in Geneva. It was a very tough call. I wanted us to spend more time together, but I didn't want to stay away from the babies any longer than necessary.

Sometimes he talked me into staying Monday night, and on a couple of occasions Tuesday, too. But while I missed him terribly, I couldn't keep away from the kids for long. I've never experienced such a fantastic pull in two different directions. I'd worry

Becki and her mother, Doris, have a baby shower at the Kmart in Bloomington, where Doris worked. The message on the cake says, "Welcome, Dilley Sextuplets."

about leaving my husband on Monday, yet feel like I should apologize to the children if I stayed an extra day in Geneva.

But that was nothing compared to my mood after the first two babies, Claire and Adrian, were discharged from the hospital on July 13. Though they weighed only a little more than three pounds, Keith and I felt confident about caring for them, thanks to the many hours we'd spent at the hospital feeding and changing them and learning their habits.

Even so, our first night away from the hospital with them, which we spent at the Indianapolis apartment, was sobering. Adrian, who was in the grip of a vicious case of colic, kept us up all night with his crying. Keith, who had never experienced this sort of sensory overload, paced around saying, "I don't know if I can handle this." He passed almost the entire night rocking Adrian back and forth and watching television.

We planned to care for Claire and Adrian in Geneva, then come back to Indianapolis when Ian, Brenna and Quinn were discharged. But by the end of the first week we knew we couldn't stay with that plan. Having my children so far apart was driving me crazy. Keith and I brought Claire and Adrian back to Indianapolis that Friday and stayed the weekend. Keith babysat at the apartment while I went to the hospital to see the other babies, then I'd watch Claire and Adrian while *he* went to the hospital.

During that weekend we spent an entire evening at Keith's parents' house, where his mom got her first really good look at Claire and Adrian. It was the second time she saw the children. The first time happened the week of the birth, when she somehow willed herself to come to the hospital, even though she was bedridden with pain and fatigue. She came by at about five P.M., with Keith's dad pushing her wheelchair. We showed her a video of the birth, then Keith took her to the nursery.

She cried the entire time. Keith rolled her chair from one isolette to the next, telling her everything he knew about each child. In spite of the fact that she was in great pain, she stayed in the nursery for a very long time. When the visit ended, her dream had been fulfilled; she saw and touched every one of her six grandchildren.

When we stopped by her house with Claire and Adrian, we simply set them down next to her on her hospital bed, which had been set up in the living room. While we played cards and talked at a nearby table, she ignored us all and got to know her two grandchildren. Occasionally she'd ask for a bottle or announce that she was going to change a diaper, but that was all.

We always believed she fought so long and hard against the cancer because she wanted to see the babies. Now that she'd accomplished her goal, she seemed to fade quickly. On July 23 we were supposed to pick up Brenna, Ian and Quinn from the hospital, but just as we were leaving Keith's aunt called, asking if we could stop by his parents' house on the way down. I said we could come by after getting the kids, but she said no—we should come right now. Guessing the worst, we drove down immediately, but Keith's mom died just a few minutes before we arrived.

Given what we faced, Keith never had a sufficient chance to grieve. The very next day we visited the hospital to pick up three more babies—everyone except Julian. Though I was counseled not to compare the babies' growth rates, it was hard not to be concerned when five babies were drinking from bottles and breathing room air, while one still needed a feeding tube and couldn't seem to catch his breath.

At least the doctors had finally discovered what held him back. Julian had a hernia, and the harder he labored to breathe, the worse it became and the more it hurt. The doctors didn't notice it at first, but as it expanded it became impossible to miss. Keith and I saw it for the first time when we came down with Adrian and Claire to visit the other four babies. We nearly keeled over at the sight of it. The hernia was as big as a baseball, and getting larger every time he cried. Obviously, only corrective surgery could end his suffering, but Julian was too weak at that moment to handle it.

On the day we picked up our other three babies, we spent every available moment with Julian. I wanted to sit all morning with him, because I had no idea when I'd get a chance to see him again. I even talked the neonatologist into letting me hold him. Keith and I traded him back and forth, then collected the other three babies and headed for Geneva.

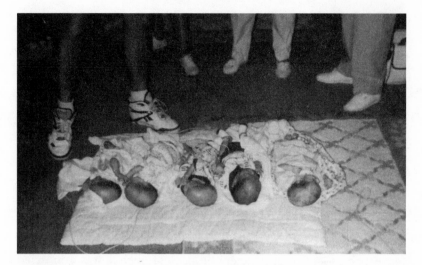

The first five children, home for the first time. We didn't allow many photographs of the family together before Julian came home because we didn't want to leave him out. This is a rare one.

The children slept better with a bunkmate. In fact, we often found that the easiest way to calm down a crying child was to put him or her in with another.

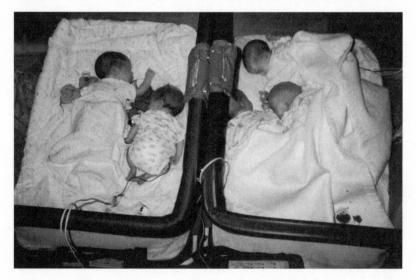

I didn't see him again during the rest of his hospitalization. It was absolutely terrible. I had five babies at home that demanded literally every waking moment of my time, and Keith and I worked to within an inch of exhaustion. We kept a photo of Julian in his crib, and I didn't allow pictures to be taken of the other five because it made it seem as if we were living our lives without him. I *already* felt that way. I didn't need any more rein-forcement.

I still received a daily phone call telling me how my son was doing—though at the time he seemed like my son in name only. The nurses seemed to bond to him more strongly than I had. It was getting very hard to take, because it seemed like I didn't even know him. I was mailed some snapshots of the nurses rocking him. It was good to see that he got the attention and love he needed, but *I* wanted to be the one giving it to him.

At least he was resting more comfortably. The doctors placed supports on his hernia that seemed to lessen his pain and ease his breathing. He put on weight, helping him build the strength he'd need to withstand corrective surgery.

But that day came much sooner than anticipated. One night Julian tore away his support truss, aggravating his injury. The hernia grew so severe that action had to be taken immediately, whether he was 100 percent ready or not.

The crisis began on August 3. During my regular morning update the doctors told me that Julian's hernia looked worse and that he would be evaluated by a specialist that day. I wasn't too concerned, since Julian was always being evaluated for one thing or another. But moments later I got a second call telling me that he might be operated on in a few days. And then, not five min-utes after that, a pediatric surgeon called to tell me that Julian

August 21, 1993: Julian comes home. To celebrate, we drove all of the children back to the hospital to accompany him. (From left to right: Keith and Brenna; Aunt Roni and Ian; Becki and Julian; Grandpa Stauffer and Adrian; Cousin Troy and Claire; Grandpa Dilley and Quinn.)

wasn't breathing well and that he needed my consent for immediate surgery.

I never felt so helpless in my life. There I was in Geneva, surrounded by five babies screaming for lunch, while my other son was being prepared for surgery more than 100 miles away. My mom and I tried desperately to find enough emergency help so that I could drive to Indianapolis, but we couldn't on such short notice. Finally Keith and I decided to simply wait by the phone, rather than risk being on the road when the surgeons called to report.

The news, when it finally arrived at five-thirty that evening, was good. Julian came through the surgery well and was recovering in intensive care. I received regular updates from the nurses caring for him. "He's just a charming little guy," one said. I think I needed to hear that.

The next day we drove to the hospital. Julian, in spite of the surgery, looked so much better that it shocked us. He'd been placed back on a respirator after the operation, but during the night he pulled out the tube and started breathing on his own. Even better, he was taking pure room air, with no oxygen supplement.

I was shocked when the intensive-care nurse casually said, "Of course you'll want to hold him." Oh yes I did. Keith and I were given rocking chairs, and we spent at least four hours passing him back and forth. For the first time he wasn't in pain, and we weren't afraid to touch him. For the first time, our fourth son was truly ours.

About two weeks later, Julian—larger, stronger and ready for the world—was released from the hospital. We cleaned out the Indianapolis apartment, said our goodbyes and took him to Geneva to join his brothers and sisters. For the first time, the new Dilley family was together under the same roof.

❀ 9 ❀

CRY, CRY AGAIN

Becki, in a creative mood and perhaps suffering from sleep deprivation, arranged this pose with her mother. Becki was amazed by how agreeable the children were to her choreography.

❀ ❀ ❀ ❀ ❀ ❀

BECKI

When Julian came home from the hospital, we finally gathered our entire family together under one roof. Only then, as we got to know our children for the first time, did we realize something important.

They weren't very nice.

I guess we had it coming. For years we'd fantasized—and I do mean *fantasized*—about what having kids must be like. Now we got a cold dose of reality. Our six babies turned out to be the most demanding, grumpy and uncooperative bunch ever to mess a diaper. The endless round of feedings, baths, changings and all-night crying stints kept Keith and me in a fatigue-induced fog during most of our first months of full-time parenting.

It didn't seem so bad in the beginning. Even our surroundings were laid-back. The babies came home to the tiny town of Geneva, an agricultural community near my dad's hometown of Berne. Geneva sits amid the flatlands of northern Indiana and is filled with broad, quiet streets lined with stately old homes. Many

Amish families live on nearby farmsteads, meaning you are just as likely to pass a horse and buggy on the country lanes as you are another car.

My parents purchased a two-story brick house complete with a large front porch, and we transformed an upstairs living room and laundry area into a Baby Command Center. We lined up six cribs along the living room's walls, then stuffed the laundry room with a rocker, microwave, TV set and enough clothes, blankets and towels to outfit a kindergarten class. We hadn't purchased much baby equipment prior to the birth, because we couldn't bear the thought of looking at an empty crib if something went wrong. Once the kids arrived, however, Keith, my mom and I snapped up cribs, toys and sleepers.

Getting ready for the babies, though hectic, was nothing compared to the stress of the previous few months. At first, Geneva seemed like a nice break from the fuss and bother we'd faced in Bloomington and Indianapolis. Little did we realize that the fuss was about to follow us to our new address.

Because the children came home in groups of two, three and one, we eased gradually into our caretaking roles. The weekend before Claire and Adrian left the hospital, Keith and I went on our last official date. We visited Geneva's tiny movie theater, where we saw *Jurassic Park* on a screen just a little larger than a bedsheet. Still, it was great fun, especially since we knew that it would be our last carefree moment for a very long time. We'd still have an active nightlife—it's just that most of it would concern diapers and feedings.

From that day forward we were still together, but never really *together*. Keith would work perhaps ten or eleven hours at his food-service job, then come home to watch the kids in the evening. As for me, I became a twenty-four-hour nanny. Ironically, things didn't seem all that bad when Claire and Adrian first arrived. Adrian cried a lot, but otherwise the two of them seemed almost eager to fall into a nice, predictable eating, sleeping and bathing routine. Every day my mom and I refined their schedule, guiding the children through the hours with almost military precision. It got so easy that we figured adding four more babies to the system wouldn't strain us at all.

But we hadn't reckoned on Hurricane Brenna. When she and her brothers, Ian and Quinn, blew into town, they trashed our carefully laid schemes. Bath time at nine A.M.? Not anymore. And no more group feedings or naps, either. The second batch of kids kept to their own, individual schedules, and they protested at the tops of their lungs whenever we tried to make them adhere to ours. Instead of the babies settling into our routine, we scrambled to accommodate theirs.

Hurricane Brenna

Adrian, a cuddlebug

Quinn. He may look like something out of *Alien Nation* here, but as you will see, he grew into his head and is much sought after by baby photographers.

About the only good news we got was that Adrian, who had been the World's Grumpiest Baby since coming home from the hospital, suddenly stopped crying. Maybe he figured he couldn't compete with Brenna's nonstop wailing, or perhaps he realized that we could no longer pick him up every time he fussed. With five babies to watch, there simply wasn't time. For whatever reason, he quit complaining, put on a smile and became one of our most agreeable, cooperative kids.

That was fine with us, because we needed all the cooperation we could get during those difficult days. Meals were a hectic affair, since we had to feed each baby fairly quickly in order to serve the entire group in a reasonable amount of time. But Quinn, whom we nicknamed Pokey, would have none of it. He slowly sipped his formula bottle, sometimes taking an hour to finish off three or four ounces. Absolutely nothing could hurry him.

Ian, on the other hand, eagerly completed his meals—and then just as eagerly vomited them up. Feeding him became a guessing game. How much could he handle before he hurled? The tension level always rose as he approached the end of a feeding. Hurl Boy would happily take every last swallow, then unload his entire lunch on your shirt.

Considering what the kids dealt with, I can understand some of their grumpiness. Julian was on a special drug to stimulate his breathing, and the rest of the babies received caffeine doses to guard against sudden infant death syndrome (SIDS). The caffeine kept them from falling into such a deep sleep that they might stop breathing. Of course, it also kept them from falling asleep easily, or resting through the night.

I also gave the babies three or four daily doses of iron supplement to counter mild cases of anemia. The iron increased their hemoglobin counts, but it also caused constipation. I had to give

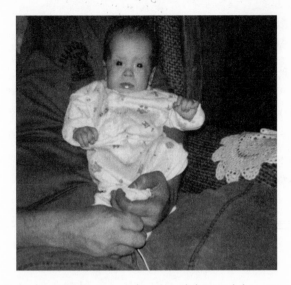

Ian. He had a sensitive stomach, so we didn't rock him too much.

the kids suppositories and keep track of their bowel movements on a chart. It was like I was a nurse again, keeping track of a ward full of cranky patients.

In spite of the disruptions, we soon settled into a new routine. Keith usually awakened at five A.M., while I got up at five-fifteen. We prepared a handful of bottles in the kitchen, then trotted up to the nursery before the babies started stirring at five-thirty. Keith helped with the feedings as he prepared for work.

After a frenzy of meals, changings and baths, by 8:00 A.M. the babies were ready for their "awake time," which they usually spent on a thick blanket on the living-room floor. They played and fussed, and neither my mom nor I accomplished much during this chaotic time.

Around ten A.M. the kids got another bottle and bedded down for their midday nap. Provided everyone cooperated and went to sleep, I could then tackle what became my second full-time job—

paying bills and keeping track of the kids' numerous doctors' appointments. Mom handled most of the housework and also visited the grocery store and ran errands. I'd eat a quick meal before the kids awakened for their afternoon snack. Then, God willing, they went back to bed for a late-afternoon nap.

When Keith came home at around four P.M., I usually turned over child-care responsibilities to him and took a one- or two-hour nap of my own. This was no luxury. Since I often got only one or two hours of nighttime rest, that extra sleep was all that stood between me and the funny farm.

Around seven or eight P.M. the babies bedded down for the night—or for whatever part of the night they deigned to let us sleep through. One or two stragglers would always refuse to close their eyes, so we'd bring them downstairs to watch TV with us until they nodded off.

And so it went, day after day and night after night. We kept so busy that I can't remember *ever* sitting down and having a half hour to myself. Our only private time was when we took showers. Poor Keith couldn't even play his rock-and-roll CDs. After listening to babies crying all day, I couldn't stand the noise. And that went for my mom's show tunes, too. Whenever either of them put on music, it was only a matter of time before I swooped down on the stereo and turned the volume control back to nothing.

And yet, even when I felt bone-weary, I still loved to hear the babies stirring in the morning. It was just like my reaction to morning sickness. The hard work, the fatigue, even the crying all confirmed the fact that I was finally a parent.

Not that Keith and I would have turned up our noses at an occasional good night's sleep. But for a number of reasons, that never happened. First and foremost, we constantly listened for

Ian

Adrian

Claire

Brenna

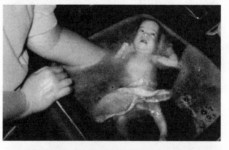

Quinn

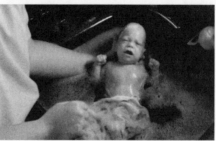

The first sink bath at home. We took turns with the honors.

alarms from the sleep apnea monitors the children wore. The machines guarded against SIDS by constantly tracking each baby's heart and respiration rates, then sounding a piercing alarm if either drifted below safe levels. If a sleeping baby didn't draw a breath for twenty seconds or his or her heart rate fell below eighty beats per minute, the machine emitted a loud beeping sound that resonated from one end of the house to the other. During those first months we received several genuine alarms, which sent the entire household scrambling for the nursery. Whenever it happened, we simply woke up the baby in question, and his or her breathing and heart rate quickly returned to normal.

Unfortunately, the monitors also went off whenever one of the electronic leads attached to the babies' chests came loose. Since the kids soon made a game of tearing them free, we faced perhaps two dozen false alarms every twenty-four hours. Though the false alarms sounded different from real ones (a steady buzz rather than beeps), they still brought us running. The buzz was loud enough to wake the neighbors, and just a few seconds of it awakened— and enraged—all the babies.

Not that Brenna, our champion crier, needed such outside motivation. She cried endlessly, never seemed happy and demanded constant attention. She crumpled her arms and legs into a tight little ball, went rigid when held and avoided eye contact. It was almost as if she dared us to comfort her.

Our pediatrician feared her stiffness might be an early sign of cerebral palsy, and prescribed range-of-motion exercises for her. For a week Keith became her full-time physical therapist, keeping her strapped to his chest in a baby carrier from dawn to dusk. He worked Brenna's arms and legs, talked to her constantly and gave her all the love and attention any child could ever want.

That attention turned her around in just one week. Brenna, we soon learned, didn't have cerebral palsy; she was just incredibly insecure and frightened. Keith's constant attention drew her out and helped her become more trusting and secure. In short order her crying tapered off and she seemed more relaxed and interested in the world.

Keith's therapy sessions also created a very strong bond between the two of them. Today, whenever Brenna feels overwhelmed or frightened, she looks for him first. I can comfort her when she cries, but Keith's the only one who can get her smiling and happy again. That week of intense interaction changed his outlook as much as Brenna's. For the first time, he told me later, he really felt like a dad.

The babies made steady progress, but Keith and I feared that our nonstop schedule might kill us before our kids learned to walk. Many times we spent entire nights picking up and rocking one crying child after another. Often we'd calm one down, lay her back in her crib, quietly creep back to our own bed—and then hear another erupt five minutes later.

We took turns getting babies at night. Usually. We spent many an evening lying in bed arguing over who got the last one. Sometimes we grew so tired that we couldn't remember if we had gotten up to take care of a baby, or only dreamed it. I also think I was conned on more than one occasion. "It's your turn," Keith would say in the middle of the night. "I got Adrian a half hour ago, while you were asleep." Right. Often we headed for the nursery together, since more than one baby usually started up at once.

Since they all stayed in the same room, letting them "cry it out" was impossible. Claire, for instance, had a cry that sounded like a cat being run over by a steamroller. The other babies would cringe when they heard it. Thankfully she was the best sleeper of the bunch, so we didn't hear her midnight air-raid siren very often. But when we did, we headed for the nursery at a dead run.

Nighttimes were also rough because the kids, accustomed to living in a bright, bustling, always-noisy special-care nursery, had trouble adjusting to the silence and blackness of true night. We solved the problem by leaving the lights on and playing a radio. The babies usually awakened to the dulcet tones of the morning farm report.

Julian had particularly fierce night terrors. On only his second evening home he woke up shrieking, triggering a bronchial spasm that kept him wheezing and screaming all night. I walked the

Claire, no bigger than a Cabbage Patch Kids doll. In fact, all of the children were wearing Cabbage Patch Kids clothes, a common wardrobe item for premies.

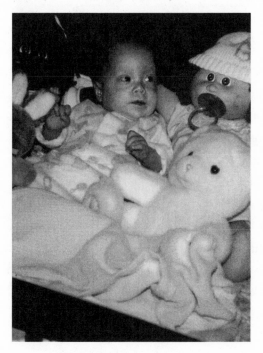

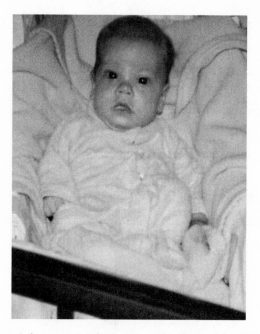

When Julian was awake, you could tell: He was all eyes.

floor with him for hours while he writhed and sweated. The spasms were basically panic attacks: He'd have a night terror and scream, which made breathing difficult, which made him scream more. At one point he had them for four nights running. The attacks were so frightening that on a couple of occasions I considered taking him to the emergency room.

It might not have been such a big deal had I been able to calm Julian down. Trouble was, he still didn't know us very well, so being held by Keith or me—two total strangers—wasn't much comfort. Plus, in such situations the parent must be calm in order to calm the baby, and I was anything but. Slowly, however, the panic attacks lessened as he grew more familiar with us and his new surroundings.

In the midst of all this, I remember my mom telling me that late-night feeding and rocking sessions were a great time for husband-and-wife talks. Well, not for us. Keith and I were usually too groggy to form complex thoughts. I mean, it's cold, it's three A.M., you've been awakened from a sound sleep and there's a screaming baby two inches from your ear. It's not exactly a Kodak moment. It would be nice to say that we had lengthy heart-to-hearts about our goals and plans for the future, but our remarks were usually confined to testy comments or simple grunting. We became experts at not waking up 100 percent during feedings, which made going back to sleep easier.

A few weeks of sleep deprivation left us both feeling punchy. Keith put in forty to fifty hours at his job in addition to helping with the kids, but I still think he had the better schedule. As he's said on several occasions, slinging hash at the amusement park seemed like a vacation compared to watching the babies.

Though my mom—and occasionally my dad and brother—helped out, the bulk of the baby work naturally fell to Keith and me. My brother was particularly good at racing up the stairs to check out apnea alarms, but he wasn't much help with diapers. All I had to do was mention the word and he'd magically vanish from the room.

Though friends from Bloomington occasionally volunteered to watch the babies, even then I couldn't make myself relax. I'd hear the kids cry and listen to make sure they were taken care of, or someone would wake me with a question. It seemed almost everyone was intimidated by the babies' size (they didn't reach normal birth weight—eight pounds—until their fourth month) and the apnea monitors. So were we, for that matter. Keith and I woke up whenever we heard a cry or an alarm, and still bounded out of bed at six A.M., whether we needed to or not. As Keith said at the time, "It's in our blood now."

Not that the babies needed kid-glove handling. They were much more robust than they looked. Only Julian, who suffered from childhood asthma brought on by the lung-scarring oxygen, had any bona fide problems. But even his prognosis wasn't bad. While childhood asthma condemned Julian to wheeze through his first year of life, as he grows older the scarring will be replaced by new, healthy tissue. While the damage might lower his breathing capacity as a baby, by the time he grows to school-age size it won't even be noticeable.

Still, the doctors told us that he would be delicate for a while, and would bear watching. During his hospitalization he received drugs that caused his bones to grow brittle, something he proved by breaking a rib shortly before leaving the hospital. I was told to make sure he didn't take the sorts of tumbles most toddlers face, because they might cause a fracture. Keith and I also guarded against any respiratory infections he might pick up during his first winter. I became so protective that I didn't start thinking about Julian as a truly healthy baby until he was one year old, free of drugs and on his way to wellness.

The only other health issue that concerned us was the possibility of vision damage from the oxygen. We made regular, harrowing visits to an ophthalmologist, who monitored the babies' retinal development. It was a nightmarish procedure, because the only way to check their retinas was to immobilize their heads in a viselike contraption, then hold their eyes open. You can imagine their reaction—and mine. It took an entire day to calm the children down after this experience.

When we weren't actually tending infants, plenty of other jobs competed for our attention. The babies each went through roughly two sleeper and gown changes each day, which worked out to a minimum of twenty-four dirty outfits—provided no one ran up the total by spitting up or having a diaper accident. We usually did two or three loads of laundry each day—barely enough to keep our heads above the dirty clothes. Given this round of chores, it's no wonder that I started seeing my daily walk to our mailbox as a minivacation. I also came to relish my occasional solo strolls to the corner drugstore for a soft drink. I looked forward to it the way most people look forward to two-week vacations.

Being housebound had one major advantage, however. We paid off all our bills and quickly brought our finances into shape. It was a breeze. As Keith said, "When you don't go anywhere or do anything, it's easy to save money."

Even the children weren't that expensive, since at that age all they really needed were diapers, sleepers, formula and bottles. Our diaper situation was completely covered, thanks to a diaper drive that a Bloomington radio station held for us shortly after the children were born. The station collected about ten thousand diapers, and the huge pile was stored in our basement, where it kept the babies dry for most of their first year. Also, strangers from all over the country sent us gifts ranging from toys to monogrammed baby bibs. And mothers of twins and triplets, perhaps out of profound sympathy, sent me their hand-me-down outfits.

Though sometimes I would have traded our entire mountain of diapers for a nap, in retrospect those early days offered some wonderful moments. Every evening we would gather around the dinner table and hold a baby board meeting. If any of the children seemed withdrawn that day, we'd make a point of giving them some extra attention the next.

We also argued over who looked like whom. As one might imagine, Keith's family initially thought all the kids looked like him, while my family maintained that they all looked like me. Eventually we decided that all the babies seemed to have my nose; my mom decided Ian looks like my brother; Claire looks somewhat like my sister; and Julian and Adrian both look like me. Quinn, however, is a clone of Keith. People marvel when they compare father-and-son baby photos.

Baths were also lots of fun, though quite draining. This was usually a two-person operation—one to bathe and diaper the kids and the other to dress them. Help was mandatory, since bathing them solo could take two hours. The babies seemed to like this ritual, especially tub baths. They also accepted sink baths, but for some reason they would not tolerate sponge baths. We learned to hate them, too, since we often ended up with six screaming infants after each scrubdown.

No doubt about it, this was a fascinating time. But as interested as we were in the children's development, the people of Geneva seemed even more fascinated—especially the Amish. While Amish women didn't consider having six babies all that unusual, having them all at once was something else. They would follow me around stores whispering to each other, and occasionally one would summon the courage to ask about the children. Once, while Keith and I were traveling with the babies, two Amish girls approached us and told us they thought I was very brave. It was a great compliment, because I always considered having childbirth *their* way—without the benefit of pain medication—to be the height of courage.

Though most folks respected our privacy, I was amazed by the number of people who couldn't keep away from the babies, no matter the circumstances. We actually had strangers knock on our door and announce that they'd stopped by to see the babies. I guess the thought of sextuplets was so novel that it overwhelmed people's sense of propriety. When we took the kids out in public, passersby would ask to hold them, something we didn't often allow, since the children's immunity levels weren't fully developed. To head off such requests, we hauled them around whenever possible in front-loading baby carriers. When people saw that the babies were completely strapped in, they seldom asked to hold them.

But a few people simply couldn't take the hint—like the tour-bus lady. One day as I paid bills, I heard the sound of air brakes out front. Figuring it was a delivery truck, I asked Keith to go outside and check it out.

"Becki, come here, please," he said nervously from the porch.

"This had better be good," I said.

It wasn't. It was a tour bus chock-full of senior citizens.

The driver got off the bus, walked to the porch and asked if we were the Dilleys with the sextuplets. We said yes, and he informed us that he was squiring a tour group through the area, and would we please stand on the porch and wave to them so that they could take our pictures? Apparently they were supposed to visit a historic building in Geneva, which turned out to be closed. They stopped at the town hall to ask about other area attractions, and some brilliant clerk told them to drop in on us.

I'm not sure why, but we consented. "This is strange, but we've done stranger things," I thought as I stood there, smiling, while dozens of shutters clicked. In retrospect, however, I'm not sure I *have* done stranger things.

After the photo op, one woman hopped off the bus and announced that she wanted a picture of the babies. Keith and I must have been in deep shock, because we allowed her to come upstairs to the nursery and see the sleeping children. We put our foot down, however, when she told us to wake them all up and place them in one crib for a group shot. Finally she settled for individual photos of each, after which I wrote down their names and birth weights for her.

My parents stifled snickers as they watched this drama unfold. Finally the woman got back on the bus, which cruised slowly around the house a couple of times so the riders could snap a few parting shots. My dad, practically hysterical with laughter, leaned out an upstairs window and waved as they drove around.

No doubt about it, life in Geneva had its moments. But such lighthearted interludes couldn't change a cold, hard fact that grew more evident each day. Living there wasn't working out. Keith operated on so little sleep that I feared he might step in front of a forklift at work. And my situation was just as bad. I would stay awake for twenty-four hours at a stretch, meaning that when Keith finally dragged himself home from work he had to take over for me immediately while I grabbed some sleep.

But what really disturbed us was the fact that he worked so hard for only a third of the money I could earn as a nurse. As the weeks passed and our energy levels ebbed, our original idea of having me work and Keith stay home looked better and better.

Finally, in early September, we made our decision. We packed up the kids and our belongings and moved to Indianapolis. I would look for a nursing job and find an apartment for us, and Keith would become the primary caregiver for the babies. After so many changes and delays, he would finally become Mr. Mom.

❊ 10 ❊

MR. MOM

Keith and Adrian napping together

❀ ❀ ❁ ❀ ❀ ❀

KEITH

Before the babies arrived, I worried about how I could possibly take care of them by myself. Now that they were actually here, and I'd seen the massive workload Becki carried, I *really* worried. At least in Geneva her mom had helped out. How could I ever handle them solo? Even worse, how could I stay on top of the housework, as Becki had?

All those things became my problem when we moved in with my dad in Greenfield. I became chief diaper changer, meal provider, housecleaner and laundry washer. I did it in the same one-story ranch where I grew up—until Becki found a nursing position and we found our own home. Little did we know that this "temporary" arrangement would last eight months.

The transition went more smoothly than any of us had a right to expect, thanks to both careful planning and luck. Money wasn't a problem. We'd saved enough cash to keep us afloat while Becki found a job, which didn't take long. Within a week she landed a full-time position as an oncology nurse, ironically at the same downtown Indianapolis medical complex where my mom had been treated.

She didn't report for her first day until two weeks after we moved—a big break for me, since it meant I wouldn't jump immediately into full-time baby care. At first we shared the work, creating a sort of baby boot camp where I learned the ropes while Becki backed me up. I needed that training, because I would be on my own quite often when she began her twelve-hours-a-day, three-days-a-week work schedule.

Of course my dad would be around in the afternoons when he got off from work, but he'd made it clear that he wanted to remain in Grandpa Mode. After spending all day installing heating and air-conditioning units in commercial buildings, changing diapers wasn't on his agenda.

Fair enough. From the start, we planned to let him do what he had always done: come home from work, sit down in his recliner and put his feet up. Still, with Mom gone, I think he took comfort from all the noise and activity. On most evenings he'd volunteer to hold the grumpiest baby until he or she settled down.

We created a new Baby Command Center in a large office near the kitchen. Becki and I lined up three cribs along one wall and deposited clothes, diapers and other supplies throughout the rest of the space. There wasn't room to set up all six cribs, so the babies doubled up. I don't know why, but they slept more peacefully as soon as we did this. Perhaps having a bunkmate comforted them. For whatever reason, we suddenly were making far fewer three A.M. nursery runs.

We also didn't miss the calf-busting stairs we'd run up and down fifty times a day in Geneva. Here, everything was next to everything else. The kitchen, dining room, laundry room, nursery and living room were all within ten feet of each other, decreasing the amount of legwork.

Our change of scenery also gave Becki and me a chance to be alone for the first time since she entered the hospital. We soon took advantage of our newfound privacy and did what any couple in our shoes would have done—we had a huge fight. It was nothing major, just lots and lots and *lots* of little things that we'd stored up over the last half year. It wasn't pretty, but it sure was therapeutic. After the argument we both breathed easier, feeling as cool and calm as the air outdoors after a thunderstorm.

But though we got our personal lives squared away, I still sweated about being left alone with the kids—as did Becki. She would be on duty from about seven A.M. to seven P.M. on three consecutive days per week. Add one-hour commutes each way plus eight hours of sleep out of every twenty-four, and she would be out of the baby-care loop for seventy-two straight hours.

I wasn't too worried about handling day-to-day tasks such as diaperings and feedings in her absence. I'd done those things in Geneva. In Greenfield I just had to do a lot more. What really scared me were emergencies. My dad's house was on an isolated country lane. If a problem arose, I was a very long way from the nearest medical facility. Plus, what would I do with the other five kids if I had to take one to the doctor? There weren't any easy answers to these questions. In the beginning we simply hoped it wouldn't happen—a vain hope, as it turned out.

While I thought I passed baby boot camp with honors, Becki still harbored doubts. Becki has always been hyperprotective of the kids, and the thought of anyone else caring for them was tough to swallow. Plus, she knew better than anyone how much work they required, and worried that I'd be run ragged caring for them by myself. It concerned her so much that she wasn't entirely sold on going back to work. "If you run into a lot of problems, I quit," she told me.

Talk about pressure.

When the big day of her starting her job finally arrived, I felt almost as much anticipation as dread. Becki's concerns about whether one person—her included—could handle the babies fired me up, and I was psyched to prove what I could do. At least I wasn't facing impossibly high expectations. I'll always remember Becki's final nervous words of advice as she walked out the door that day: "Just keep the babies alive," she said. "That's all I ask."

I had something a little more grandiose in mind. I decided that those kids would be the cleanest, most well-fed, most carefully changed, thoroughly rested babies in the *world*.

I set to work before Becki cleared the driveway. I must be the luckiest house dad on earth, because the kids were almost frighteningly cooperative. About the time I took over their care, they entered one of the most pleasant, cooperative stages of their young lives. Only a few weeks earlier it seemed they were always upset, but now even Brenna stopped crying. They smiled and cooed all day, and nothing seemed to upset them—at least, not for long. Even their physical stage worked in my favor. They still couldn't crawl around and get into trouble, yet they could hold their own bottles, so that I didn't have to cradle and feed each one.

Handling the kids was easier than I had any right to expect. Even housework wasn't too tough. The trick was never to let anything, such as dishes or laundry, stack up. When you're running a nine-person household, things get out of hand very quickly.

I tried, so far as the babies would allow it, to stick to a feeding and nap schedule. During their morning and afternoon play periods I let them motor around the living room. At first they did precious little motoring, since all they could do was roll over, lift themselves up with their arms and make feeble attempts at crawling.

Though giving them a rattle or a choice seat under a Sesame Street mobile was usually all it took to amuse them, they weren't always so pleasant. Keeping six babies happy when you only have two arms can be tough, but I had an important ally: six wind-up mechanical swings that could placate even the grumpiest kid. Sometimes I'd have four, five, even six going at once. I'd run from one to the other, rewinding the rocking mechanisms as they ran down.

Other baby-maintenance tasks weren't terribly complicated. They were just time-consuming, because I had to do them six times. Changing diapers was once a hang-up for me, but I got over it in Geneva. You can get over *anything* when you do it a couple of thousand times. Becki and I tried to change everyone's diaper every three hours (though some kids got faster attention if they suffered a particularly messy or fragrant blowout).

Baths were also fairly straightforward. In the beginning we used the sink, but after a few weeks we tried a new, two-person approach. I would fill the bathtub with a couple of inches of water and get in. Then Becki would bring me one baby at a time and we'd have a bath together. The kids loved it, though after perhaps two hours in the tub I was slightly cleaner than I needed to be. Becki called me Prune Man after this ritual.

Meals required a bit more ingenuity, particularly after the kids started eating solid food. Feeding them one at a time was out of the question. If I'd done that, breakfast would have dragged on until noon.

Instead I grabbed the two hungriest babies (as determined by who cried the loudest) and put them in pumpkin seats on the kitchen table. Then I'd open two jars of baby food and feed them both at once, alternating babies. When I saw an open mouth I put food in it. When that mouth closed, I'd move on to the other.

This system worked fairly well, though it seemed like one of the other babies always started crying before I could finish with the first two. Well, tough strained bananas, kids. It's never too early to learn patience.

Adrian and Ian were extremely patient, which meant they were always last in line. Adrian was often dead last—not necessarily a bad thing, since he got held the longest and enjoyed the least-rushed meal. But woe to anyone who failed to give him the attention he'd waited so long for. After cooling his heels all morning he expected a cuddle after eating, and if he didn't get it he'd put on a face so pitiful that it ran a knife through your heart. Even worse, he never seemed mad at *you*. It seemed as if he thought *he'd* done something wrong.

At least no one dawdled over their food. They couldn't eat fast enough—and I gave it to them pretty fast, believe me. I'd give them one bite and, like baby birds, they'd instantly want another. Poor timing was their only downfall. The kids were new to spoon-feeding and hadn't mastered the technique. They opened their mouths tentatively as I loaded up a spoon and moved it toward them, only to shut their mouths just before the food arrived. A little later, when their first baby teeth came in, they bit down on their spoons and refused to let me pull them out. It was as bad as trying to get an old shoe from a dog.

In spite of a few missteps, I knocked Becki's socks off during that first week on my own. When she walked in the door after work the babies were bathed, fed and dressed in fresh outfits; the house was immaculate; the laundry clean and folded; and dinner sat on the table. Of course, after proving my skills during those first few days, I became a little less anal about having everything perfect—especially the laundry. I still hated folding things. On many nights Becki came home to find a pile of clean laundry in the living room. The two of us would usually sit down on the floor and fold it together.

The kids didn't seem to mind—or even notice—our role reversal. It probably wasn't that big a deal from their perspective. Becki was home and helping out for four days out of every seven, and she was still around for most of the babies' daily rituals. Becki and I believe in putting the kids to sleep together and waking them up together in the morning. It gives them some comforting moments that they can always count on.

Mornings were—and are—my favorite part of the day. Becki and I wake the kids up together, and in Greenfield we even sang a corny little song that Becki made up: "Good morning, good morning, the sun shines this morning. It's a happy day." The kids smiled when they saw us, and hearing that song got them twisting around like worms. Julian stretched endlessly and grinned, the girls opened their eyes and giggled and Quinn—who was always instantly wide awake, without so much as a yawn—hauled himself up the side of his crib and jumped up and down. It made us feel great—like we were the best things in the world.

I think we looked forward to those morning wake-up calls as much as the kids did. When Becki started working the night shift, I tried to delay getting the kids up until she got home.

While having a new primary caregiver didn't seem to change the babies' outlook, it certainly altered mine. Becki says that kids get smarter by sucking the brains out of their parents. After caring for the kids, I think it's true.

Like most parents, Becki and I have trouble sustaining adult conversations—basically because we have so few. I seem to have the biggest problem, because while Becki talks to adults at her job, my most meaningful daily discussions usually center on bodily functions. Becki says I also throw tantrums. When she does something that doesn't meet with my approval, I'll stamp my feet in frustration. Well, what can I say? I hang out all day long with people who expect immediate gratification, and it rubs off.

That fall and winter I grew ever more comfortable with my Mr. Mom role. Becki did most of the cooking, primarily because she liked it and I was lousy at it. I could make an acceptable dinner, provided it was a frozen pizza. Becki also handled the grocery shopping, another task I loathed.

Even with all we had to do, the workload wasn't a crushing burden. I wasn't putting in ten-hour days at an outside job, as I had in Geneva, and Becki's schedule left her free for more than half the week. Plus, Becki and I reached a gentlemen's agreement not to be quite as obsessed about cleanliness as we had been in Geneva. Up there, we threw receiving blankets in the wash if a baby so much as looked at them. Now we took a slightly more relaxed attitude.

Not that we were slobs. After all, we were guests in my dad's house and had a responsibility to keep it up. But even those jobs seemed easier because everything was so convenient. Midnight feedings were a breeze, because the refrigerator and the microwave were right outside the nursery—as was *I* on most nights. Our bedroom was too far away for me to hear the kids, so I usually slept on the living-room couch.

Actually, that's not the only reason I slept there. Becki and I used a full-size bed at my dad's house, not the queen-size model we were used to. Ordinarily a full-size is fine for two people, but during our months of enforced separation we had both become incurable bed hogs. We delivered more elbow digs and kicks during the night than you'd see in a martial arts movie. Until we could get a larger bed, staying on the couch was a safety precaution.

We had plenty of safety concerns with the kids, too. Since my dad's house was never officially baby-proofed, we constantly watched for potential problems. That job got tougher as the babies learned to crawl. When that dark day arrived, we quickly learned to keep a constant eye out for Quinn, who started opening and closing the doors of the living room end tables. Brenna also developed a consuming fascination with the kitchen garbage can.

That newfound mobility complicated our sleeping arrangements for the babies, because they began crawling all over each other. Actually *one* baby crawled over everyone else: Quinn. One of our smallest kids, he was also the most precocious. He learned to crawl long before the rest of the kids and then ran roughshod over whoever was trapped in a crib with him. Adrian was his favorite target. He lay there like a lug and cried while Quinn pinched his nose and played with his ears. Quinn, who had no idea what he was doing, smiled sweetly while he tortured his brother. We started calling him the Bad Seed.

Adrian drew the most abuse because it took him the longest to learn to crawl. Even if Quinn had the run of the entire living room, he seemed to make a point of crawling right over Adrian, who was a sitting duck: While the other kids roamed the living room, he'd rock back and forth on all fours as if frantically searching for first gear. Not everyone was such an easy mark. If anyone so much as *thought* about invading Claire's space, she uncorked one of her famous shrieks, stopping the other baby in his or her tracks.

One of our biggest hassles was making sure everyone got along with our other baby, Winston, our now full-grown corgi. Our cat,

Ed, remained in Geneva until we found a permanent address, but Winston had the run of the house. He was sweet-tempered and harmless. Our biggest worry was that he'd drown the babies in slobber.

He wouldn't hurt the kids, but he was a mortal threat to their possessions. He routinely mistook rattles and teething rings for chew toys, quickly dismantling anything that came his way. The kids began throwing him their teething rings, which Winston would instantly crush, spraying the colored liquid they contained all over the carpet.

Eventually such hijinks became too much to bear. Rather than leave him at the mercy of six toddlers, an inhumane fate for any dog, we gave Winston away to another family. We couldn't give him the attention he needed, and the kids wouldn't give him a moment's rest.

Sometimes I knew how he felt. Though the babies were remarkably well behaved, there were moments when all six got mad at once and refused to be comforted. On those occasions, with the sounds of angry babies ringing in my ears, I fantasized about having a regular job, with only one unreasonable, demanding boss instead of six.

Whenever that feeling swept over me, I'd lie down until it went away. I reminded myself that I wasn't a career-oriented, job-comes-first kind of guy. I took my work seriously, but I didn't obsess about it. Besides, I couldn't handle another job on top of the one I already had. The pay wasn't great, but the fringe benefits were outstanding.

One of the best perks was being able to wear anything I wanted to work. Most days found me running around in a reasonably clean camp shirt and a pair of shorts. But I never let my personal hygiene slide. After a day of getting puked, drooled and pooped on, I felt so gross that I couldn't wait to jump into the shower. Plus, changing so many diapers made me feel as if I was up to my elbows in them. I'm well on my way to becoming an obsessive-compulsive hand washer.

I still toy with the idea of fulfilling a longstanding dream: growing my hair long and cultivating a ponytail. I've never done it, fearing that people would start asking who that hippy was lurking around the Dilley sextuplets. Usually Becki cuts my hair, often buzzing it so short that people ask if I'm in the military.

Still, my early days with the kids weren't always a breeze. Though I had my daily schedule licked, I never quit worrying about what I would do in an emergency. I finally found out that December. It was a bad month for Julian. He caught cold, as did all the babies, but instead of getting the sniffles like the others, the illness settled into his chest.

He suffered bronchial spasms all month, attacks so severe they landed him in the hospital for three days. On Christmas Eve he suffered a particularly bad one. I could usually ease his breathing by employing a bronchial spray similar to the inhalers asthmatics use, but that night I gave him three treatments with no change. After struggling for hours, he turned blue and went limp in my arms.

I knew I had to do something. But just as I was about to decide between sending Julian to the hospital in an ambulance alone, or else taking him myself and leaving Dad in charge of the other five babies, luck intervened. Becki's sister stopped by and stayed to watch the other kids while I took Julian to the emergency room. I spent five hours at the hospital, but Julian turned out to be fine.

That crisis made me feel more, not less, secure about my new role. After that incident we formalized our emergency procedures, enlisting neighbors who could help us care for the babies

Becki was in the Halloween spirit, so she arranged the first of what would become a Dilley tradition: the holiday theme photo.

on a moment's notice. That way I could go to the hospital while Becki rushed home from work to watch the other kids. So far, thank God, we've never had to call on them.

But the most important thing that Becki and I learned during our stay in Greenfield was that we could handle the kids by ourselves. We can't foresee every crisis, but we realize we can adapt to whatever comes up, be it a severe diaper blowout or another medical emergency. Whatever it is, we're ready for it.

11

IT'S A LIVING

At first, the children were easy to pose. They were like potted plants. But here, they were starting to get restless and were able to crawl off the couch.

❀ ❀ ❀ ❀ ❀ ❀

BECKI

Sometimes I feel like I'm a different person than I was before the pregnancy. During my childless days I spent six years as an evening shift oncology nurse, working from three to eleven P.M. five nights a week. I obsessed about my job. During workdays I cleared my schedule after eleven A.M. so that I could mentally prepare for my shift. I was also an "early" freak, showing up perhaps twenty minutes before I was scheduled to report in. And if there was an after-hours project, count on me.

As Keith well knows, I also obsessed about my patients, taking their problems home with me and hashing them out with him. It got so bad that I dreamed about the people I tended.

What a difference sextuplets make. Instead of being early for everything, now Keith and I run so late that we say we operate on Dilley Time, our own system that usually runs about thirty minutes to an hour behind real time. I'm so busy with the kids that on workdays I leave myself just enough time to jump into my scrubs, dash out the door and race to the hospital. I'm usually on time, but I'm never, *ever*, twenty minutes early.

I'm still devoted to the care of my patients, but only while I'm at the hospital. After my shift I don't have enough space in my brain to obsess; I've got six other people to worry about.

I first became aware of this transformation shortly after I returned to work. When we moved to Greenfield I scoured the medical facilities in nearby Indianapolis for job leads. Thanks to news coverage of the sextuplets, many of my interviewers already knew of me—not that this was an advantage. I cringed when people recognized my name. I could almost hear them thinking, "Six babies—bet she'll miss a lot of work."

One woman at a nursing home I phoned asked, "Are you the one who had those six babies?"

"Yes," I said, sensing a problem. "But my husband's going to stay home with them."

"I see," she responded. "Does your face look better than it did when you were on TV?"

I didn't bother showing up for that interview.

Finding a job was easy. I landed a position at downtown Indianapolis's University Hospital only a week after I started my search. Returning to work, however, was difficult. I had already thrown myself heart and soul into the day-to-day care of the kids. Sure, it was exhausting, but I *loved* it. I enjoyed watching them grow, and I didn't want to miss any part of their lives. I feared I'd begrudge every minute I spent away from them.

During the days before I started work, I helped Keith adjust to his full-time dad duties. I wasn't in the best of moods, both because I dreaded leaving the kids and because I couldn't imagine how Keith could singlehandedly manage a job that had run both my mom and me ragged.

Given my own experience, I had no idea what to expect when he took over. On my first day of work, the minute I reached the hospital I found a pay phone, called home and asked Keith how he was doing. I don't know what I expected, since I'd only been gone an hour. Keith calmly informed me that no, the house wasn't burning down: The kids were napping and he was watching TV.

As it turned out, all my fears about Keith's parenting skills were groundless. After the first week or two I started thinking he was better at the sheer logistics of parenting than I was. In Geneva, I often got carried away with watching the babies. I'd stop my chores to play with them and then, a half hour later, realize it was mealtime and I hadn't prepared any bottles.

Not Keith. He gave the children plenty of love, but he also kept to a strict schedule. He broke down each day into a series of tasks: laundry, feedings, dishes, etc. Whereas I might get sidetracked by a cute expression, Keith focused on the day's chores the way Marines focus on taking a beach. Since he was alone, no other approach would do. If he slacked off, he'd shortly find himself knee-deep in dirty laundry and hungry kids.

After seeing Keith in action, I never doubted that the kids were in good hands. It was good to have that worry off my mind, because my new job gave me plenty of other concerns. I worked in University Hospital's bone-marrow transplant ward. The facility treats patients aged sixteen to forty who require marrow transplants as part of their aggressive cancer treatments.

Working there was difficult, because many patients didn't survive. Still, I was an experienced oncology nurse who had worked with both AIDS and terminal cancer patients. I never questioned my ability to handle it.

In retrospect, I should have. The only way to deal daily with death is to keep your emotional distance from the trauma around you. It sounds callous, but it's essential to medical workers' mental health. Those who don't are quickly ground to pieces.

I soon realized I could no longer remain detached. When I went back to nursing after having the babies, I was a different person. I'd been through a lengthy hospital stay, and I knew what my patients felt. I knew how frightening it was to lie in a hospital bed and wonder what was going to happen next. Plus, we had just lost Keith's mom to cancer.

But worst of all was watching the mothers of twenty- to thirty-year-old patients and wondering what I would do if Claire or Quinn ever found themselves in such a place. My heart went out to these mothers so much that it hurt. I cried all the way to and from work. I simply couldn't handle it. I quit after only six weeks.

A few days later I got another position at a northside Indianapolis hospital, where I undertook both a new, much less harrowing assignment and new hours. I signed on for a five-day-a-week evening shift, from three P.M. to midnight, in the cardiology ward. The new hours were a vast improvement over working overnight, to which I never fully adjusted.

Any nurse will tell you that the only way to survive the night shift is to keep the same hours all week long, so that your internal clock adjusts to the upside-down schedule. But if I had done that, I would have seen the kids only when they slept. Therefore I spent half the week staying up all night and the rest struggling to readjust to a day schedule. In my previous, University Hospital, job, falling asleep during my drive home had become a regular occurrence.

I like the afternoon hours so much that I've kept them to this day. About the only thing I miss is the babies' raucous afternoon playtime. That's when the kids, for some reason, usually display their newest tricks. Whenever a baby took his or her first toddling steps, it was almost inevitably in the afternoon. The next day they'd do it in front of me and I'd say, "Keith! Quinn's standing!" to which he'd reply, "Oh yeah. He was doing that yesterday."

Walking out the door at two P.M. is like leaving a great party just as it's hitting its stride. The boys are running around, Brenna is sitting on Keith's lap, Claire is talking to herself—and I'm putting on my coat and grabbing my car keys.

Needless to say, I'm prone to occasional bouts of homesickness while on the job. Each evening I call Keith once or twice to get the scoop on who's doing what to whom. I also carry regularly updated photos of the kids in my wallet. They help satisfy the endless requests from patients and other nurses to see the babies. Plus, staring at them picks me up when I'm feeling stressed or blue.

Even better, I find they can melt the hearts of even the grumpiest, most uncooperative patients. Not that I constantly press photos of my children on total strangers. Usually by the time I meet new patients, they've been told by the day-shift nurses to ask how many kids I have. Not that everyone is charmed. One man looked at a group photo and said, "You sure played hell with the population explosion."

Even the patients who didn't know I had six babies probably sensed something was afoot—especially when I fed them. Accustomed to serving food to the children as fast as they could handle it, I unconsciously did the same thing to my patients. I finally realized what I was doing when one of them, between mouthfuls of soup, indignantly asked me to slow down.

But even though I knew that the babies were well cared for and that we sorely needed the money I earned, I still disliked not being home with them. I'd dreamed of motherhood for most of my adult life, and now it seemed like I was missing it. Plus, sometimes I felt like a slacker. Compared to raising six kids, nursing is easy. I felt terribly guilty taking breaks or resting during slow times. I kept wondering what Keith was up against at that same moment.

Even comments about Keith set my teeth on edge, fairly or not. Whenever someone praised him for shouldering the burden at home, I could sense the part they left unsaid: "What a great guy . . . why couldn't *you* handle it?" All that praise got old. It made it sound like it was the most amazing thing in the world that a man could handle the same burdens women have faced— usually without praise—since the dawn of time.

I used to tell people that Keith was a full-time dad, until a patient quipped, "So I guess you're a part-time mom." It was just a silly, offhand remark, but it cut so deeply that I excused myself, went to the women's restroom and cried.

Often I came home from work deeply frustrated and feeling incredibly inadequate. I finally made my peace with the problem by realizing that this was just one of the many sacrifices parents must make for their children. If one of our babies needed a kidney, neither Keith nor I would think twice about giving one of ours. My working was the same thing. I'd like to stay home with the children, but I can't. I will sacrifice what I want for the greater good. If that's what's necessary, then so be it.

On the flip side, for every person who thought Keith was Superman because he took care of the babies, there was another who thought they'd be safer locked in a closet than in the care of a man. Sometimes, when I told people that Keith watched the kids, they'd offer a noncommittal "Uh-huh," as if they knew that in a *real* crisis, Mom would be called in. Well, contrary to popular belief, males aren't genetically incapable of caring for children.

They are genetically incapable of changing the toilet-paper roll, but they can handle kids just fine.

I think Keith and I proved that point early on, when I didn't have to take vacation days to help with the children or come in late because of a crisis. Keith could handle everything, even emergencies, and by doing so he lightened my load at work.

My evening shift hours also made life less complicated. I left the house at two P.M. and usually got home a little past midnight. I always felt great coming home. The first thing I'd do was sneak into the nursery and watch the babies. I'd tuck their blankets under their chins, and if one seemed to have trouble sleeping, I'd pick him up and take him into the living room to sit with me.

Keith got mad when I did this—after all, he'd just finished laying them down—but what can I say? When they opened their eyes and held out their arms to me, I couldn't resist. To this day I do this. When I've had a stressful shift, sometimes I need to hold someone or something. When Keith doesn't feel like cuddling, well, I've got six other cuddly things close by. And if they're all asleep and I can't bring myself to wake them, then there's always the cat.

After I look at the kids, Keith usually serves up a fifteen-minute report on what happened while I was gone. I usually ask him some penetrating questions, like "Did they do anything cute today?" We often discuss Claire's emotional state. She's the queen of mood swings, and when she's angry she can ruin *everyone's* day. As for Quinn, he's usually done something either very brave or new.

And then we go to bed. I no longer dream about my patients. I'm concerned about them while I'm working, but when I leave the hospital I move on. It took a long time for me to stop making that emotional investment, but I think I'm a better nurse for it.

The next Dilley holiday theme photograph, at Children's Museum in Indianapolis. We were surprised Santa could get all six children in his lap.

Claire

Ian

Adrian

Quinn

Julian

Brenna

As I learned from personal experience, giving too much to your patients can be devastating.

These days I make my emotional investments closer to home. Occasionally I get off work a few hours early, and if it's past the kids' bedtime I may run a few errands. Usually I pick up something for Keith, either restaurant carryout or his favorite snack, doughnuts. Keith thinks I do this so I can have a few moments to myself. That's only partly true: I don't want to escape from him or the kids, but I enjoy slipping away from the relentless scheduling that rules our lives. I can roll down the car window, listen to my favorite radio station and enjoy the sound of my own thoughts.

But those thoughts never stray far from Keith or the kids. And it isn't long before I steer a course for home.

❖ 12 ❖

FAIR HOUSING

By November 1993, it was hard for us to hold three children at once.
Becki's group was happier . . . this time.

KEITH

❀ ❀ ❀ ❀ ❀ ❀

KEITH

Taking care of the kids at my dad's house was fairly easy. All we lacked was a secure play area. We let the babies run around the living room, but someone watched them every second. As they became better crawlers, this job got tougher. Quinn in particular made it his personal mission to explore every available drawer, door and shelf.

When the babies were on the floor, Becki and I watched them like prison guards, ready to serve up some quick "No's" or jump up and retrieve anyone who scampered out of our line of sight. It was no fun for the babies and certainly no fun for us. The kids needed their own space. We *all* needed our own space.

But when we looked at apartments, we came up empty. Building managers were pleased to see us—until we mentioned that we had six children. Visions of oatmeal-stained walls and irate tenants complaining about the noise must have flashed through their heads, because they suddenly seemed a lot less interested.

Usually we were told that the two-bedroom units we wanted were far too small for such a large family (never mind the fact that the kids' cribs could easily fit in one room). We'd need, we were advised, at least four bedrooms: one for us and three for the kids.

Not a chance. The rent for something that large would exceed the monthly payment for a four-bedroom *house*. Plus, given the damage six babies can do, we figured we'd never see our deposit again, either.

Instead we looked into buying or building a house. We first considered a very modest prefabricated model (about the only thing we could afford that would give us enough space). Then we discussed the problem with Jane Elliott, a client representative with the Indianapolis law firm that represented Becki, me and the babies.

We'd hired the firm shortly after the babies were born to handle (and more often, deflect) media requests for interviews. Besides dealing with everything from Japanese news programs to American grocery-store tabloids, the firm also dealt with baby-products manufacturers interested in giving us samples of their wares. Given the huge strain that six kids put on our budget, we were more than happy to make arrangements with reputable companies. But *only* reputable ones. While we turned down $50,000 from the *National Enquirer* for rights to the babies' story, we happily accepted six car seats and high chairs from a local manufacturer, Cosco.

Most of those early deals were for desperately needed, very pricey items. We received one of the most wonderful offers from a formula maker, Enfamil. Each month a semi would pull up to our house and unload a month's supply of their product. Becki and I didn't get rich off such deals, nor did we want to. They simply kept our expenses within tolerable limits.

When we told Jane about our troubles in finding a place to live, she offered to investigate what sort of deal she could put together on a house. We figured we might get a break on the price, but we never imagined anyone would *give* us a house.

As it turned out, we did far better than we expected. Jane found a custom builder who was willing to put up a house at cost. This was more than a business deal to him. The builder and his wife had struggled through fertility problems similar to ours, and he was very excited about working with us. He didn't even request any promotional considerations in exchange for his work—no "I built the home of America's only sextuplets" TV commercials.

His company even redesigned the standard two-story home plan we selected to make it more kid-friendly. "I always tell couples not to build houses around kids because they grow up and move away," he told us. "This is the very first time in my career that I've broken that rule."

Did he ever. The two-story loft that was supposed to soar over the kitchen–great room area was cut into two stories, with the extra upstairs space used to create a large playroom. The utility room was also moved upstairs into a niche adjoining the kids' area, and two extra bathrooms—one for the boys, one for the girls—were installed.

Downstairs, the kitchen-dining area was expanded by about three feet to make room for six high chairs, and wall space in the kitchen was freed up to accommodate a very large refrigerator. The house also included an extra pantry.

We were extremely grateful for all the consideration we received. That's why we still wince over the fiasco that disrupted our mid-March closing. Becki and I thought we had everything worked out: We would leave the kids with sitters, dress in our finest and appear at the mortgage company's glass- and brass-filled offices as the very models of respectability.

Not exactly. Only a few hours before we planned to leave, our sitters begged off. That left us only one option: take the kids along. We quickly dressed the babies and packed them in the van, then took off in the midst of a driving rainstorm for Indianapolis. We arrived with only seconds to spare. I jumped in the back of the van, pulled kids out of their car seats and passed them to Becki, who belted them in their strollers. I worked so fast that I didn't notice that Ian had suffered a major accident in his diaper. Or, more accurately, everywhere *but* his diaper.

Not realizing his condition, I hauled my poop-covered son out of his car seat, dragged him across my clothes and then handed him to Becki, who did the same thing. Before we realized what had happened, we were both coated head to toe in very fragrant baby doo-doo.

After a brief but extremely heated discussion about why I didn't notice this in time to save our outfits, we changed Ian's clothes, wiped ourselves off as best we could with baby wipes, tried to collect our wits and headed for the entrance. The receptionist looked at the babies and said, "How cute." Then she looked at their distracted-looking, poop-stained parents and tactfully averted her eyes.

The kids, for obvious reasons, were by this time nervous, hungry and screaming their heads off. They needed bottles and diaper changes, and after some hesitation we were directed into the only available area, the company's plush meeting room. We quickly changed and fed the kids, dumping the dirty diapers into a large plastic trash bag that we dragged around during the rest of the proceedings. I began wondering if the moneymen might take one look at us and back out.

A few minutes later the contractor and the attorney handling the closing joined us. There was no place for the babies, so they roamed around on the floor while we completed the paperwork. Quinn kept taking off the attorney's pumps and carrying them away. Usually closings take at least an hour, but I think the sight of the kids drooling on the carpeting, along with the pungent odor of our clothes, sped things up. We were done and out the door in twenty minutes.

Compared to the closing, moving was a breeze. Movers hauled over most of our furniture the Tuesday of the next week, and the kids came over that very day. They were surprisingly well behaved, considering the upheaval they faced. We kept corralling them in different rooms, depending on where the movers were. If they were moving boxes into the upstairs bedrooms, then we'd herd the babies down to the empty dining room and hem them in with portable baby gates.

I put together both our bed and the six cribs—our only major goal for the first day. Four of the cribs went into the larger of the babies' two upstairs bedrooms. The boys would sleep there. A smaller bedroom closer to our master suite was turned over to the girls. The babies not only had to adjust to new quarters, but to sleeping in separate cribs in two different rooms.

Inevitably, no one got much sleep that first night. We put the babies to bed at around seven-thirty, then spent the next hour trying to settle them down. I felt for them, because they had a lot to contend with. We played their favorite lullaby tapes, but the rooms' unfamiliar acoustics made them sound so different that they weren't very comforting.

Finally we simply closed the bedroom doors and left them to work it out—which they did, after much whimpering. I'd decided before the move to adopt a strict sleep-all-night rule at the new house. Though on several occasions I practically had to tackle Becki to keep her from visiting the babies when they cried, within a few days all was quiet from bedtime till dawn.

Becki and I faced our own adjustments. We hadn't slept in the same bed for more than a year, and were dealing with a problem we hadn't faced lately—the fact that both of us snored. We spent most of our first night together elbowing each other and saying, "Roll over, you're snoring." But just like the kids, after only a few tries we were sleeping through the night. We'd lie on our sides until we went to sleep, then roll onto our backs and make enough noise to drown out a sawmill.

For the next three days we worked around the clock getting everything unpacked and stowed away. With six kids to watch, we feared that if we didn't handle everything immediately we'd still have packing crates in the living room six months later. The babies quickly adjusted, and thrived, in their new surroundings. Even Ian, who takes the longest of any of the kids to adjust to new things, settled in.

After months of moving around, we finally found ourselves deep in the bosom of suburbia, living on a cul-de-sac with a high backyard privacy fence to keep in the kids. It was a safety-conscious parent's dream. Our next-door neighbor was even a policewoman.

The Dilley family was finally home. The kids had plenty of room to play, and even Becki and I had our own private preserve: the upstairs suite. It's off-limits to the kids, and I think we'll keep it that way until they're a little older—say, thirty.

Shortly after we arrived, we strapped the kids into their strollers and rolled them around the neighborhood. The babies loved it, and they made a wonderful icebreaker with strangers. We quickly met most of our neighbors and got plenty of babysit-

Valentine's Day theme shot, February 1994. We want each child to feel like an individual, so we don't dress them in matching clothes, except on very unusual occasions.

ting offers from teenage girls, many of whom dropped off their computer-generated résumés and rate cards at our house.

I'm not sure we'll use their services anytime soon. We figure we'll need two or three sitters to handle so many babies, which means an evening at the movies for Becki and me could cost us as much as a one-way ticket to Florida.

Maybe we'll stay in for a while. We don't have cable and we don't rent many movies, but we're rarely bored. We've got our own entertainment center upstairs, in the playroom.

✸ 13 ✸

THEIR OWN
LITTLE WORLD

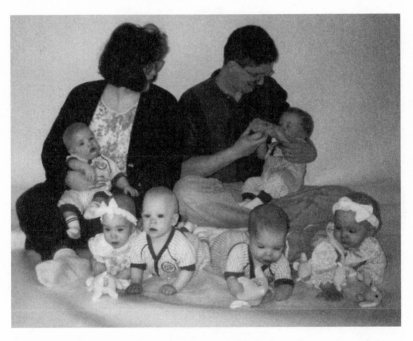

When we play with the children, everyone is usually in a big pile.

❀ ❀ ❀ ❀ ❀ ❀

BECKI

Once the babies adjusted to their new surroundings, the fun really began—both for them and for us. They had the run of most of the upstairs, including the spacious boys' bedroom and the playroom just outside. They motored all over that teal-carpeted area, allowing Keith and me to sit back and watch them interact on their own terms. It was almost like watching a nature show: *Mutual of Omaha's Baby Kingdom.*

The upstairs playroom was separated from the stair landing by a baby gate. The room itself was loaded with toys, along with a small mattress under two windows where the kids could take breathers. There was no furniture (to inhibit unauthorized climbing) save for a TV set and VCR, where the kids got their daily *Sesame Street* fix.

The best thing about this new, far more secure setup was that we rarely had to interrupt the babies' escapades with a "No." The area was meant to do two things: safely entertain the kids and absorb punishment. The walls were painted a washable white, and the carpet was low-pile and treated to help prevent stains. The kids dripped everything from baby formula to drool on it. Keith, the vacuum freak, really indulged himself here.

The festivities usually began around seven A.M., when the babies started stirring. Often we'd hear Claire talking to the stuffed seal in her crib, or else making ga-ga noises at Brenna. The two of them would sit facing each other with their legs sticking out between the rails of their cribs. Not all wake-up calls were so cute, however. Once Claire called us out of bed by dragging her tiny fingernails across the wall behind her crib, producing a sound as annoying as fingernails on a chalkboard.

Almost no one cried in the morning. The girls were happy to see us and even happier to see their brothers. Usually we woke them up and diapered them first (primarily because they were closest to our bedroom), then let them toddle in to see their siblings. Adrian almost always greeted us with an ear-to-ear grin, while Quinn jumped up and down on his crib mattress, to the amusement of both us and the other kids.

Once everyone was changed and fed, the kids spent the balance of the morning either playing upstairs or in the first-floor great room. The noise level was fantastic. It just didn't seem possible that six tiny babies could cause so much racket.

It was especially awesome when we listened to the thudding and thumping from downstairs. It sounded as if they were moving pianos around. About the only thing that could settle them down (or stun them into submission, depending on your views) was the TV. When Keith or I put in a videotape, all playing and talking instantly stopped. The kids plopped down on their bottoms and didn't move until the end of the show. This was so effective we started calling it Video Valium. About the only thing that upset them was when Quinn, who watched Keith intently and quickly learned the purpose of the "eject" button, shut off the tape.

While TV pacified the kids, music energized them—or enraged them, depending on what we played. Keith is a rocker, but I'm afraid we've spawned a houseful of easy listening fans. The babies cried at the sound of music videos. We also learned, thanks to Keith's misguided attempt to broaden their musical horizons, that they *really* hated the heavy metal band Metallica.

The babies preferred classical music, the Beatles, the South African group Ladysmith Black Mambazo and R&B—particularly Aretha Franklin's *Respect*. When they heard it they started dancing. Quinn, our most coordinated, would shuffle his feet, run around the room, yell "Ahhhhhhhh!" and then stage-dive onto Keith or me. Adrian, our other dancing machine, marched around the room laughing.

Although we usually stayed with the kids during their upstairs play periods, we felt confident enough about their safety to leave them alone for short stretches. During the early days they could barely manage a slow crawl, so we figured they couldn't get into much trouble. Keith took advantage of such lulls to work on the housecleaning.

One of the biggest ongoing tasks was keeping the playroom carpet from getting too soiled. To cope with the problem, for Father's Day I got Keith the most powerful, attachment-laden vacuum cleaner I could find. It vacuums, it shampoos, it does everything but windows. The only drawback is that the children were terrified of the noise and cried whenever they heard it. For that reason Keith usually vacuumed while they slept.

We watched the babies more closely as they learned to stand and then walk—and then *scheme*. On one occasion Keith walked out of the boys' bedroom, came back a moment later and found Claire standing on the windowsill, looking out the window. We haven't a clue as to how she did it. All we know is that the kids all developed a mania for climbing, and would use anything, including each other, as footstools.

That drive to climb soon forced us to remove most of the upstairs furnishings. The chest of drawers in the boys' bedroom went as soon as the kids started pulling out the drawers and using them as climbing perches.

When it came to adventure, these babies knew no fear. About the only thing (besides the vacuum cleaner and Metallica) that really rattled them was isolation. They loved to swing the door between the playroom and the boys' bedroom back and forth, and occasionally one or two unlucky ones would swing it all the way closed, cutting themselves off from the rest of the group. They instantly became hysterical, as would the babies on the *other* side of the door. I guess they just couldn't handle being separated.

Adrian was the worst perpetrator. We'd watch him play endlessly with the door, swinging it back and forth until he finally shut himself in. Then we'd open it, he'd settle down, play with the door some more—and shut himself in *again*. Even worse, the locked-in kids often lay down and threw fits directly in front of the door, making it hard for Keith or me to push it open.

Besides the door, plenty of other nontoys grabbed their attention. Early on they fell in love with a bright yellow plastic laundry tub, which they sometimes sat in but more often flipped upside down and used as a drum. Three or four of the boys would hammer on it at once, making more racket than a marching band on contest day.

Keith's navel was another point of interest. For some reason the kids became fascinated with it, and would pull up his shirt to look. Actually they were fascinated by Keith and me in general, which led to the creation of one of our favorite baby games: lying on the floor and letting the kids swarm all over us. It was a riot to have all those babies use us as human jungle gyms, though we usually sustained a few twisted ears and pinched noses in the process.

But while this game was fun for us, the babies hated receiving similar attention. Once Claire got stuck under a mobile and started crying. The other babies promptly surrounded her, sat on her and started touching her face. By the time I reached her, Claire—not the most mellow child under the best conditions—was livid with rage. She was in no danger, however. I don't think her siblings were being mean. Her crying worried them, and this was their idea of helping.

Fortunately, the babies stopped crawling over each other and "piling on" shortly after we moved from Keith's dad's house. All the babies had become competent crawlers, and they were too mobile to get run over. Plus, shortly after the last stragglers learned to crawl, Brenna took her first steps, followed by Claire and Quinn.

At first Brenna was shy about standing in front of an audience. But when she really wanted to get somewhere she'd stick out her tongue, hoist herself up on two legs and take off. When Claire wanted to walk, she'd stick her fanny way up in the air, stand and then look to us for a reaction. Often she got so excited that she'd plop right back down on her fanny.

This falling-on-the-fanny thing got to be a habit. Keith and I soon realized that much of the noise emanating from the play-room was simply the babies bouncing down on their rear ends.

As the kids' mobility increased, so did the size of their domain. During the spring we let them explore the backyard. A privacy fence kept them from escaping, so they could safely tear from one end of the property to the other. They would take off across the grass, then suddenly stop and turn around to make sure we were still there. If they couldn't spot us instantly, then we'd hear squalls.

Besides running, the babies chased rubber balls, let Keith or me haul them around in a wagon or splashed in a baby pool filled with a couple of inches of water. Claire, ever her own person, liked to just sit on the grass and look around—usually while the boys ran back and forth chasing their shadows.

Play time was almost always fascinating. Actually, fascinating isn't a strong enough word. In the early days I would watch the kids giggle and play, turn to Keith and say, "It's too cute in here. We may need to leave for a few minutes." I wasn't kidding. When the kids were on their best behavior, watching them could trigger an overdose of the warm fuzzies.

Fortunately (I guess) the babies usually kept those warm fuzzies in check by pulling some terrible stunt or getting into a bad mood. First they'd be the picture of cuteness, then five minutes later they'd all start fighting over the same toy.

Right now we can solve most of these crises by cuddling the injured party and putting the perpetrator down for a mandatory nap. I hope they behave better as teenagers, or we may have to *keep* them in the playroom—though we'll need a much higher gate.

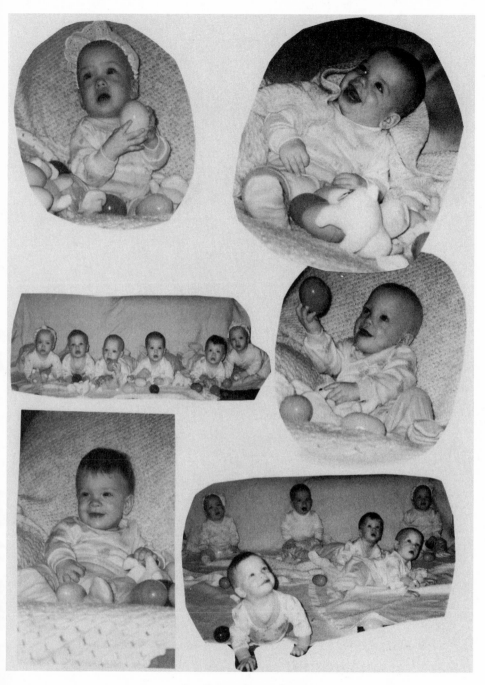

Our Easter theme shot

❀ 14 ❀

GROUP DYNAMICS

Becki's personal favorite photo. Claire and Adrian were just laughing, sharing some secret when we caught them.

❀ ❀ ❀ ❀ ❀ ❀

KEITH

A few weeks after our move, a nationally recognized home baby-proofing expert visited us on behalf of the National Child Safety Council. A company associated with the council planned to donate the necessary gear to make the house safe for the kids. On the basis of the expert's advice, we installed everything from plastic bumpers on the corners of the great-room fireplace to special doorknob rings that prevented the babies from turning them. We even crawled around on our hands and knees to see the world as our kids did.

The advice and the equipment took a load off our minds, but we still kept a constant eye out for the kids. That's because while most baby-proofing items easily withstand assaults from only one child, they fare less well against six. Especially *our* six. As toddlers our kids boasted a combined weight of 120 pounds. When they went somewhere or did something as a group, no child gate or doorknob guard could stop them.

Quinn and Adrian, who were bunkmates. This is how we found them, giggling one morning after a nap. The birthmark on Adrian's forehead will fade by the time he's three.

Julian and Quinn. At this age, they were the most mobile and would crawl on the other babies. We put them in the same crib, so they wouldn't wake up the others.

Ian and Quinn, eating lunch in the playroom. They often pick up cereal and feed each other.

Ian and Quinn sharing a *very* rare moment. Usually Quinn is on the move while Ian is studying something quietly. Here they are playing with a toy milk container and, thankfully, not fighting over it.

Claire is generally the gatekeeper of her toys and doesn't always let the other children in. Here she makes an exception for Julian.

Quinn, on the verge of being able to walk, in May 1994. We would soon know what it's like to have six mobile children.

Becki and I realized what we were up against only a few days after moving. The kids were playing upstairs while we cleaned house downstairs. The hall from the playroom to the stairwell was gated, and another baby gate stretched across the top of the stairs.

These seemed like adequate precautions for kids who had only recently mastered crawling. But then we heard a gigantic thump that sent us scrambling up the stairs. When we reached the playroom we found the babies lying on top of each other in a heap, with the gate on top of them. Apparently they all approached it at once, grabbed hold and pulled backward. The gate, which wasn't meant to cope with such an assault, collapsed.

Today it's funny, but at the time Becki was shaking with fear. Fortunately the kids were too startled—and too tangled up in each other—to make good their escape. They just lay there and cried while Becki and I sorted them out.

At least they wouldn't have gotten far. The stair gate still blocked their path, and it was anchored into the wall with drywall screws. They could never have gotten past that. I *think*.

Worrying about such things gave us the willies—and pointed up how different caring for six babies could be. Plenty of people have raised six kids, but the fact that ours were all the same age presented special problems. Normally, we could have used the older ones to help us watch the younger ones. But in our case, it was just Becki and me against Team Dilley.

Once we realized the difficulty of tracking and containing so many kids, we took baby-proofing even more seriously. We were advised, for instance, to get rid of the medium-size bucket I used for mopping. Babies, we were told, can fall head-first into them and drown.

At first such possibilities seemed a bit far-fetched. I remember glibly saying that I didn't make a habit of saving my dirty mop water, and that the babies wouldn't be allowed underfoot while I mopped, anyway. But then I realized that our kids could be in six different places at once. With so many babies running around, just a few seconds of brain fade on my part could lead to tragedy. Once Becki and I realized this, silly-sounding things like toilet guards (clips that lock down the lid) became more than middle-of-the-night nuisances. If they served their purpose once, we reasoned, they'd earn their keep.

But all the toilet guards and fireplace bumpers in the world sometimes couldn't cope with the kids' sheer unpredictability. For instance, the babies liked to open and close the door between the boys' bedroom and the playroom. They also liked to pull on it, and one day they did it so much that they came within an inch of yanking it off the wall.

That's right. By acting together, six toddling babies pulled so hard on the full-size door that they ripped out six of the nine dry-wall screws securing the hinges. They were close to removing the last three when I discovered them. I reinstalled the door with three-inch screws, which I figured should hold them off until kindergarten.

At least they weren't consciously working together. Not yet, anyway. Whenever something like the gate incident happened, we figured the babies had accidentally done the same thing at the same time. By the time they're old enough to *really* act as one, we hope to use that very group behavior, in the form of peer pressure, to help them behave.

We've already taught the kids to do many things as a group. Though as infants they all kept their own schedules, as they grew we worked hard to introduce eating and sleeping schedules. We tried to determine each day's milestones, striking a balance between rigidity and flexibility.

As always, we changed everyone's diapers every three hours. But even with this predictable system, changings could be an adventure. We never knew what we'd find when we opened those bedroom doors. Quinn became a veritable poop Picasso, removing his diapers in the middle of the night and painting both his crib and himself with the contents.

Thank God for disposable diapers. Becki and I consider ourselves environmentalists and we worried about our very large contributions to area landfills, but what could we do? We couldn't survive without them.

We briefly considered switching to cloth, until we tried them briefly while the babies recovered from diaper rash. That was a black time. We double-diapered every kid, but they were constantly soaked, as were their beds. I became a human laundry machine, tossing in load after load just to stay even with the carnage. Even worse, we couldn't just throw away the dirty diapers. We had to *save* them in a hamper. That hamper soon became a bigger environmental disaster than any landfill.

We returned to disposables as quickly as possible. Becki and I make a conscious effort to recycle what we can to conserve our kids' environment. By recycling formula cans, baby-food jars and other household metals, glass and plastic, we have cut down to four bags of trash weekly.

The rules for sleeping were similar to diapering: Everybody went to bed and got up at the same time. Waking the kids up was fairly easy, since early risers seemed content to play quietly in their cribs, and late risers usually snapped awake the minute we walked in the room.

Bedtimes were often messier. The kids usually went down between eight and nine-thirty P.M. It all depended on when they started fussing. Generally, we wouldn't let only one cranky baby send everyone to bed, but as soon as we got two whiners, it was bedtime. Everybody was carried to their cribs, the lights went out and in short order all was still.

Feedings were equally straightforward. Though Brenna seemed to favor sweets, by and large the kids weren't picky eaters. That went double for Adrian, who will probably someday earn the nickname Tank because he's so much larger and stouter than the other kids. Adrian eagerly accepted almost anything edible that came his way. I can't imagine the food bills he'll generate as he grows. Our family meals will look like an NFL training table.

Lunch usually took place in the six high chairs clustered around the kitchen table. The babies also took snacks there, including one of their favorites, torn-up Pop Tarts. When Becki and I served this treat upstairs, the kids clustered around like pigeons and let us pop pieces in their mouths.

Quinn and Claire were our most impatient eaters, finishing their food in a flash and then struggling to extricate themselves from their high chairs, either by crawling over the trays or slipping under them. What did we do when those two troublemakers wouldn't sit still while the others finished? Why, exactly what any parent with six babies would do: We let them get down. In a perfect world this might have been a great opportunity to teach discipline and patience. But our world isn't perfect.

We didn't sweat such small stuff. We *couldn't*, considering our workload. If Quinn wanted to get down and run around while the rest of the kids finished eating, so be it. Letting him go was less disruptive than spending the rest of the meal trying to keep him in his high chair. And if he had food on his face but we didn't have time to clean him up that instant, then we'd get it a little later. This wasn't textbook procedure, but it worked. With six kids and only four arms between us, we soon realized that some standard child-care methods just didn't cut it.

But that wasn't always the case. Becki found herself applying many of the same childrearing rules that her own mom had used on her. Becki is a Dr. Brazelton fan, and believes in letting kids be kids, rather than picking on them constantly for every minor infraction.

As for discipline, we became great believers in giving kids "time out." The technique worked like magic during the babies' first year. If, on occasion, a baby grumped around for a long time for no good reason, we put him or her in a crib. Usually they fussed briefly, fell asleep and woke up half an hour later with a much-improved outlook. And whenever *everybody* acted up, all Becki and I had to do was make our voices slightly more firm. They picked up instantly on the change of tone and usually modified their behavior.

Of course, we seldom resorted to such measures because tiny babies aren't exactly hard-core discipline problems. As they get older, however, I think it will take a lot more than a simple change of tone to control this mob. Already they look at us twice when we tell them no. To most of the kids, "No" seems to mean "Stop what you're doing for ten seconds, until I look away."

Becki and I figure that once the kids get older, they'll start putting stuff over on us left and right. After all, they outnumber us three to one. We hope to even those odds by making extensive, unabashed use of peer pressure. Given what we're up against, it may be our only chance for maintaining day-to-day discipline. For instance, if Quinn won't stay with the group when we go to the mall, then we won't go out, and trust the other kids to show Quinn the error of his ways. It's either that, or go around with whistles around our necks for the next two decades.

As those trials approach, I hope we remember that we can't be perfect. In parenting, doing a good job is enough—and probably all that anyone has a right to expect of mere mortals. The kids, we've realized, aren't just a part of our lives. They *are* our lives. We just have to do our best and then hope for the best.

❀ 15 ❀

THEY'VE GOT...
PERSONALITY

The first pool shot, in our new backyard, August 1994. We didn't want to put too much water in the pool, figuring that six children would displace most of it.

❀ ❀ ❀ ❀ ❀ ❀

BECKI

After months of watching our babies grow, Keith and I realized something remarkable. Our parents always told us they knew us better than we knew ourselves. Now we knew they were right.

Though we'd never believed it as teenagers (who does?), we saw the truth as soon as our own children arrived. We learned that caring for a baby gives parents front-row seats to the formation of a unique human psyche. Our first year with the kids was like a baby orientation program, with courses such as Brenna 101, Advanced Julian and Developmental Ian.

Those classes were very informative. With each passing month the babies' unique traits solidified. We could count on their acting in certain familiar ways, ways that soon became second nature to us. Sometimes they stepped out of character, but by and large we knew who was vulnerable, who was outgoing and who was patient. We knew how they would react to almost anything—and I have a feeling we always will.

Brenna loves people. She's always the first to sit in someone's lap. If someone falls down, she comforts them. And she wants to know what everyone else is doing.

Here's what the children have taught us so far.

Brenna, though she possesses an incredibly annoying cry, is also one of our most loving children—at least on good days. When she's nervous or unsure of herself, she's our clingiest baby, sticking close to Keith and me for support. She loves to sit on our laps and she gives us more kisses than any of the other kids.

I've never seen her be mean to the others. Occasionally she'll take a toy from someone, but she doesn't do it as a provocation: She just wants to look at it. And she's never slapped or even yelled at another child. If a baby takes a toy from *her,* she plops down on the floor and whimpers. Then she'll run to either Keith or me (usually Keith) for comfort.

Not so with Claire. She's tough, assertive and the devil herself if crossed. If they ever make a preschool version of *Dynasty,* she could play Alexis. When she's good, she's wonderful. But when she's bad, run for cover.

Claire doesn't take much guff from the other kids. Instead, she dishes it out. If someone gets in her way, she'll scream loudly and angrily. And heaven help anyone who makes off with something of hers. She'll pursue them from one end of the playroom to the other until she gets it back.

And yet, after a busy day, she'll come to Keith, smile sweetly, lie down on his chest and fall asleep. She can be incredibly charming when she wants to be. But while she's a tough customer with the other kids, she melts around animals, especially Ed. Unfortunately, Ed seems to dislike her, and runs away every time she tries to cuddle him.

Adrian, on the other hand, is living proof that the biggest aren't necessarily the meanest. Though he's almost twice Claire's size and far larger and more sturdily built than the other babies, he never throws his weight around. He's as jolly as a little Santa Claus, grinning constantly and dishing out his good-natured laugh. It's good that he's so mellow, because if he keeps growing at this rate he'll be playing football for Notre Dame before sixth grade.

Claire, in a charming moment

Adrian, sweet-natured and jolly

Right now, however, he's more interested in taking the path of least resistance. He's so easygoing that when he was born he didn't want to be weaned off the respirator. There wasn't any medical reason to assist his breathing. It was just . . . easier.

Not surprisingly, Adrian doesn't cope well with adversity. If he stumbles or falls, he cries until everyone knows what happened. Once either Keith or I comfort him, he smiles and goes about his business. But until he gets a reassuring hug, he puckers his lower lip and pouts.

While Adrian takes life as it comes, Quinn grabs the gusto. He's a budding Type A, and the only baby who routinely stands up to Claire, whom he easily matches in both fearlessness and precociousness. He's always been smaller than the other kids, yet he was the first to crawl and one of the first to stand and walk. His size disadvantage probably pushed him to excel. Quinn could never be as easygoing as Adrian. You can only do that if you're big. Quinn was little, so he had to work harder.

The little guy keeps looking for new challenges, be it climbing to the top of the dresser in the boys' bedroom (we stopped him before he got too far) or mastering new toys. He's absolutely fearless and almost immune to bumps and bruises, but he also desperately wants to please Keith and me. During playtime he's forever handing us things. And when he's not off looking for the next mountain to climb, he snuggles up next to us.

We dread disciplining him, though not for the usual reasons. If we say no to Quinn, his lips pucker and tremble and his eyes tear up. Seeing that spirited little guy look so crushed hurts us as much as him. When he puts on that face, sometimes I just have to look

Quinn, looking like he's ready for high school

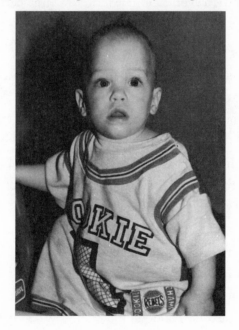

Ian, introspective and studious. He'll be the one holed up with the computer.

away. I've even overlooked a few minor transgressions because I couldn't bear to watch him pout.

Ian is our most private baby. He was the last to crawl, the last to stand and the last to walk, so for the longest time his lack of mobility put him at a disadvantage. He'd throw a ball and crawl after it, only to have it snatched away by someone faster. Instead of pursuing the other baby or yelling angrily, he just sat down and cried.

He's also an incurable cuddle bug. When the playroom gets too loud and rowdy for his taste, he often appears at our side, wanting to be held. He's also very moody—one minute literally jumping with joy, the next despondent and crying. When he's groggy just before bedtime, he'll sometimes laugh and cry in the same breath.

Of all our kids, Julian is the one I dote on the most. I think I'm still trying to make up for leaving him alone in the hospital for five weeks. If all the kids start crying, I usually go to him first. And if anyone gets picked up and rocked after bedtime, it's him.

Julian returns that attention a thousand times over. Now fully recovered from his earlier medical problems, he's usually very happy and has a cute sense of humor. If he sees something funny he'll burst out laughing, and sometimes he'll walk around giggling for no apparent reason, as if he just told himself a great joke.

But when he turns south, step back. When one of the babies takes something away from Julian, we can hear his wail throughout the house. He's even worse than Brenna, because he cries continuously. But the minute someone holds him, he shuts it off like a light switch, settles down and gets happy.

Julian. Here he's sober, but he's usually the entertainer in the family.

Not surprisingly, during their first year Claire and Quinn were inseparable. They shared toys without fighting and displayed a common love for finding new challenges. They were always the ones to try something new and impressive. On the other hand, if anyone pulled out a dresser drawer, broke a toy or emptied the contents of a closet onto the floor, it was them.

The rest of the babies preferred running around with each other over hanging around with Mom and Dad. That was a relief, since we weren't sure what we'd do if they all rushed us at once, craving to be held.

Most of the time a couple of kids sat with us until they felt satisfied, then wandered off and were replaced by others. Even Quinn and Claire occasionally toddled over. But in typical Type A fashion, they tried to push or pull whatever baby we were *already* holding off our laps. They'd latch onto their hair or shirts or just give them a good, hearty shove.

The kids didn't seem to mind not being held constantly. Even when they were infants, they rarely fussed for more attention. I think that from their earliest days they knew not to waste their energy complaining about the arrangement, because nothing could be done. About the only time they got grumpy was after visits from relatives, when they were held much more than usual. They quickly developed a taste for it, and protested mightily when the visitors departed and things got back to normal. We called that particular malady Arm Withdrawal.

The babies coped well with visitors, though they usually needed time to adjust. They didn't get too many guests in the upstairs playroom, so whenever someone new stepped not very gracefully over the baby gate into their domain, they froze in their tracks and gazed at them wide-eyed, soundless and absolutely immobile, for perhaps fifteen seconds.

After the initial shock they quickly loosened up. Brenna, the most nervous of the bunch, was often the first to approach newcomers—once she felt safe. But Quinn, ordinarily Mr. Adventure, didn't cope well with visitors, especially if Keith and I weren't around to make introductions.

Things got rough, however, if the babies were outnumbered. More than six visitors at a time made them nervous and withdrawn. One weekend we invited about two dozen friends and relatives over, and they all trooped upstairs to look at the kids. Big mistake. The babies were overwhelmed. They huddled together in the middle of the floor, shaking.

Brenna, as usual, took it the hardest. I picked her up, but she kept gazing frantically around the room for Keith, who was outside. Finally I had someone go get him. As soon as Brenna saw him her arms went out, as if to say "*There* you are."

Often the way we reacted to stressful situations determined how the kids behaved. For instance, whenever someone sustained a minor boo-boo, the first thing the injured party did was look at us. If we seemed concerned, they usually cried. Needless to say, we soon learned not to overreact to routine bumps and bruises. If we smiled and said, "Did you go boom?" the injured party usually smiled and forgot about it.

Because the kids got along so well together, we were less worried than most parents about the terrible twos. Mothers of other multiples told us that because the kids have so many built-in playmates, they don't pine for attention as single 2-year-olds would.

I also learned that multiples sometimes develop their own language that only the siblings understand. Their own *language*?

Hmmmm. The thought of my six kids conspiring in code worried me. But then I realized that they could talk to each other in Mandarin Chinese, for all the good it would do them. I'd still know what was up. Like my parents before me, I know exactly what makes my kids tick. After all, I was there when they wrote the instruction manual.

❋ 16 ❋

ON THE ROAD

Keith can take a nap almost anywhere—on toys, on the floor, in the rocking chair. But he's always keeping an eye on the kids, or at least keeping an ear open. Becki says it's like living with a human cat.

❀ ❀ ❀ ❀ ❀ ❀

KEITH

Like many married couples with lots of relatives, Becki and I used to spend most of our Christmases on the road. We'd drop in on her parents, then open presents with my family, then visit friends. Often we didn't get home until late that evening.

Not anymore. These days anyone who wants to see the Dilleys on Christmas will have to come to us. The thought of taking six kids out on icy roads in subzero weather makes me cringe. For us, there's no place like home for the holidays.

Actually, the thought of taking these kids *anywhere* jangles my nerves. I don't expect to feel better about it anytime soon. Loading the babies, pacifying them en route and then keeping track of them once we arrive requires careful planning, split-second timing and all the patience, and muscle, Becki and I can muster.

At least we have a great transportation system. We travel in a gigantic twelve-seat van that was practically given to us by a local car dealership shortly after the babies were born. Even when fitted with six car seats, there's still enough room for diaper bags, strollers and Becki and me. If it weren't for the van, we'd need a convoy of cars for trips.

Still, traveling is usually an adventure. As you can imagine, walking around with six babies tends to draw crowds. We've got nothing against large gatherings, and if I weren't the kids' father I'd probably stare, too. It's just that it's hard to shop or run errands when you're constantly ringed by onlookers.

We first realized the depth of this problem in Geneva, when Becki and her mom took the kids for their first pediatrician appointment. Somehow the local papers got wind of it, and reporters and onlookers bushwhacked them when they arrived.

We've always tried to cooperate with the media, but this was too much. The kids had gotten immunization shots and were in a foul mood—hardly a great moment to conduct interviews. Becki's mom is a private person and she had a tough time handling the attention.

We certainly sympathized, especially when we realized we couldn't take the babies out in public without causing a scene. Like any parents we're happy to talk about and show off our kids (just try and *stop* us). But drawing an audience when we're busy either loading them in the van or taking them out is excruciating. Just imagine how hard it would be to care for your children if a crowd of strangers got to watch—and make comments. After all, we're not the Brady Bunch. We're just a mom and dad trying to do the best we can in an extraordinary situation. We make mistakes just like all parents. Unfortunately, we sometimes make them in front of audiences.

We faced one of our worst experiences when we first moved to Greenfield. We took the babies for their immunizations, and I made the mistake of parking next to a crowded farmers' market. As soon as we started unloading the kids more than a dozen women surrounded us. All of them seemed to think they could handle the kids better than us.

As we unloaded, someone said, "That one's too cold! Look how cold her hands are."

Becki, though obviously perturbed (to say the least), said the kids were fine, and that we'd put blankets on them as soon as they were secure in their strollers. We kept working, but a moment later the same woman piped up again. "Oh, her hands are cold," she said of Claire. "These kids are not dressed at all. They're premature babies and they're going to freeze." Then she leaned over Claire and said, "Your mom wants you to get pneumonia."

Ordinarily I let such comments roll off my back, but now even *I* got steamed. Becki, who like any mom is sensitive to criticism of her parenting skills, started shaking with annoyance. "I'm getting tired of the comments from the peanut gallery," she whispered to me.

Just as it seemed things couldn't get worse, they did. As Becki put a blanket over a stroller full of babies, her purse slipped off her arm and boinked Claire on the forehead, triggering one of Claire's hair-raising crying screams. Becki wanted to die.

As for me, I was ready to kill. Unbelievably, the same woman who had carped about the blanket opened her yap once more. "Look at her!" she said to the crowd. "Mommy smacked her in the face with her purse."

In spite of the provocation, we set our jaws and walked away. Though we've never again felt so thoroughly cornered, we still get lots of unsolicited comments—not all of them positive. Most are good-natured queries that we're happy to answer if time and circumstances permit. But certain people think nothing of asking the most personal questions, like how much Becki weighed while pregnant, or whether we plan to have any more kids. At least I have a snappy comeback for that one: "Not until we sell these."

Hitting the road with six babies requires careful attention to detail. We first check the weather to see how to dress the kids. If it's cold, we spend ten to fifteen minutes putting coats and hats on everyone. The babies hate hats, except for Claire, who seems to associate wearing them with going bye-bye, which she loves. By the time we finish dressing the last baby, the first is already hot and complaining and has likely tossed his or her hat God knows where.

Loading the van is far less complicated. First we pack enough bottles, diapers, clean clothes and baby wipes for the trip, then load them in bags and stow them onboard. We take all the things any parent of a single child would—just lots more of them.

Next I break down and load the kids' strollers, then start the van and let it warm up. Finally, Becki and I each grab babies and take them outside. Becki stays in the van and belts the first two kids into their car seats while I head back to the house for more. This bucket brigade continues until everyone is strapped in. Then I pile into the front seat, while Becki sits in the last of the van's three rows, where she can watch all the kids. The loading process usually takes about ten minutes—but only if we stay focused.

Still, no matter how quickly we work we can never move fast enough for the kids. Usually the first two babies we load in the van get tired of waiting and start crying. We don't worry about it, however, because things usually get *very* peaceful once we start rolling. As any parent knows, a moving car affects babies the same way a sleeping pill affects adults. The kids look out the windows for a few moments, babble to themselves and then nod off.

The babies stay content for as long as the van keeps rolling—or until their rears get numb, whichever comes first. But woe to us if we stop. Claire even cries if we slow down. She must have some sort of internal speedometer, because it seems like she whimpers if we drop from sixty to fifty.

While I drive Becki plays flight attendant, making sure everyone stays comfortable. No one gets in-flight refreshments, however, because the car seats won't let the babies lean back far enough to take bottles. To feed them we have to park and remove them from their seats, an inconvenience we try to avoid, since it can double our travel time. Normally we'd give all the kids bottles at once, but in the van we can only unstrap and feed two at a time, often while the other kids howl indignantly. Usually we plan trips so that we reach our destination before the next scheduled feeding.

The kids can go three to three and a half hours without a diaper change or a bottle. But though they're excellent travelers, they're lousy arrivers. The babies wake up and start crying the minute I kill the engine, and they keep crying while we unload them and belt them into their strollers.

But as soon as the strollers start moving, they quiet down, settle back and enjoy the ride. Naturally, Becki and I strap them in as quickly as humanly possible. On a good day it takes about fifteen minutes to extract the strollers from the van and reassemble them, then transfer the kids from their car seats. I usually try to park at the far end of parking lots, to attract the least amount of attention.

Most of our early trips were from one secure location to another, say, from our house to my dad's house, or from our house to the pediatrician's. Given the logistics and work involved, we didn't have the nerve to load up the kids, go someplace public and just . . . hang out. Something unexpected might happen, and when you're shepherding six babies, you dread the unexpected.

For a couple of months we had trouble taking the kids *anywhere*, let alone on a joyride. As the babies grew we needed three twin strollers to transport them, which meant we could only take them out if we got someone else to help. We solved the problem when the babies were six months old by acquiring a gigantic four-seat stroller.

I assembled the monster on our living-room floor, surrounded by curious babies (including Quinn, who tried to eat the instruction manual). It was as long as a golf cart. The kids sat in tandem, with the front seat perhaps a foot off the ground and the last, highest seat almost as high as my chest. The staggered seating gave it the profile of a drag racer, and it was so carefully balanced that I could steer with one hand. I could even pop wheelies, which the kids enjoyed.

There was only one drawback. The machine grabbed almost as much attention as the babies. We might as well have hung a sign over it reading, HERE COME THE DILLEYS. Plus, it still wasn't big enough for all our kids. Whenever we went out, we took along a supplemental two-seat stroller. The most placid kids rode with me in the four-seater, while the squirmiest or grumpiest sat in the two-seater, which Becki handled.

Now that we had all the necessary equipment, we figured we had no excuse not to take the kids out more often. In early spring of 1994 we decided to visit a large home and garden show at the Indiana State Fairgrounds. We planned to leave in the late morning, but by the time we bathed the kids and dressed them in their Sunday best, it was already past three P.M.

I broke down the four-seat stroller and shoehorned it into the van. As we drove down the driveway, Becki and I made a solemn vow: If either of us started feeling antsy about taking the kids out in public, we'd abort and go home.

Well, there was plenty to be antsy about. We got lost on the way and almost ran out of gas. Then the kids picked up on our stress and began whimpering. And when we finally reached the fairgrounds we were shocked by the massive crowds. Plus, a nagging all-day shower suddenly turned into a cold, driving rain.

For several minutes we sat in the van, trying to decide what to do. Then Becki noticed something. "Where's the handicapped entrance?" she asked. "We need to find a ramp so we can get the strollers in."

It must have been somewhere, but we couldn't see it from our parking spot—and there was no way we were going to unload the kids and run around in the rain looking for it. Then, as if on cue, Claire launched into an eardrum-busting tantrum.

That was that. I fired up the van and we headed for home.

But while we shied away from our first group expedition, that didn't mean the babies never got out. If Becki ran an errand, she often took along one kid, whom she strapped into our car's single car seat. Some made better traveling companions than others. Quinn was too squirmy to hold, and he wormed out of the safety seats mounted on grocery-store carts. Claire was a breeze, primarily because she sits so quietly—though she's not above pitching an occasional screaming fit in the middle of the produce section.

The best thing about going out with only one baby was that you didn't draw attention: You were just another parent and child. The kids enjoyed it too, because they got one-on-one attention. Adrian loved his first trip to the grocery store with Becki. She went up and down the aisles so he could look at the colors and she took things off the shelves for him to handle.

An eight-month-old baby probably shouldn't be amazed by the grocery store, but what could we do? We had neither the time nor the stamina to take the kids out as much as we wanted. Becki still worries that if they don't get more of a taste of the real world, they'll have no social skills when they enter kindergarten.

No doubt about it. Sometime—sometime *soon*—we have to get the kids out into the world more. But it won't be fun, and it will get worse as time passes. At least now we can belt them into strollers and keep them all in one place. What will we do in a few years, when we go someplace and they take off in a half dozen different directions?

It's enough to give a house dad nightmares. Still, we can't hide inside for the rest of our lives. Maybe we'll visit public areas, like malls, only during slow times so we can't draw crowds. Or maybe we'll confine ourselves to kid-friendly places like parks, the zoo or the local children's museum.

Or maybe we'll take the suggestion of a family friend who now lives on the East Coast. The thought of taking the babies there for an extended visit made us nervous, until she offered an excellent suggestion. "I've got it all worked out," she said. "I'll have six T-shirts printed with the name of a fake day-care center or kindergarten, we'll put them on the kids and people will think it's a field trip."

Crazy? Maybe—or maybe not. To a man with sextuplets, the line between crazy and brilliant sometimes gets very blurry.

❁ 17 ❁

THE HIGH COST
OF DILLEYS

The children getting ready for a swim. Becki is trying to give them pool-safety tips, but she doesn't think they understand. At this point, the children could still be carried down the stairs two at a time.

꙰ ꙰ ꙰ ꙰ ꙰ ꙰

BECKI

Shortly after the kids were born, a rumor circulated that the state of Indiana had given me and Keith one million dollars for having sextuplets. I still occasionally hear that story, along with the assertion that we got our new house for free. Rather than dignify this strange tale with a denial, I offer a standard reply: "If I have all that money, why am I still working?"

If only it *were* true. Still, I'm not sure that even one million could handle our expenses, not at the rate our kids go through food and clothes. Given our needs, a million dollars probably wouldn't last through their teen years.

At first the kids were fairly cheap. They didn't need much formula, we had free diapers and their wardrobe consisted of dozens and dozens of inexpensive sleepers. But as time passed, their needs grew. Even the most incidental things strained our budget when multiplied by six. Take baby wipes, which cost three to four dollars per eighty-four-sheet container. That's reasonable— unless, like us, you go through perhaps four boxes a week, pushing the cost to around thirty-five dollars a month. Economy brands cost less, but since we usually need two or three sheets to accomplish what the best brands do in one, we don't save money.

Thank heaven toys are not a problem. During the babies' first birthday our friends and relatives showered them with enough gifts to keep the kids happy through kindergarten. Our only toy-related difficulty is finding places to store them all.

I wish we could say the same for food. At twelve months the children were like an ever-growing, ever-hungrier gorilla. Among many other things, the gorilla needed two gallons of milk, one gallon of juice, almost an entire box of cereal and—appropriately—six bananas each and every day. Once we took the gorilla to a restaurant, where it polished off two quarter-pound hamburgers, three large orders of fries and two dishes of ice cream.

Our food bill soon became as big and as frightening as King Kong. Once our biweekly grocery tally seldom topped $70, but by the end of the kids' first year I spent around $225 per month for food, with no end in sight. I already pile our cart to the top each and every time I visit the supermarket. Before long, grocery store runs may become two-cart, two-person affairs.

The babies could demolish a large, economy-size can of ravioli in one sitting. Adrian, who was usually served first because he was least patient, often polished off his helping before I finished serving the others. To meet this ever-rising demand, we're sticking to the basics: in-season vegetables, canned goods and bulk packages.

Once we considered purchasing entire sides of beef and using them for months, but after seeing the kids in action I think we may have been optimistic. Keith has said we'll buy sides of beef, but we may just throw them over the playroom baby gate and jump back.

Ian's got rhythm.

Claire at bath time

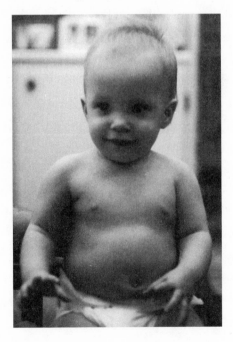

At least the kids weren't picky during their first year. They enjoyed green vegetables, so we packed them with as many as possible while that happy state of affairs lasted. They particularly liked peas and became great grilled-cheese fans. About the only thing they rejected were hot dogs. I chopped up five of them into baby-size pieces one day, but the kids wouldn't touch them. Keith wound up having hot dog hash for lunch.

As the kids got bigger, our wallets got thinner. Keith, who tracks our expenses with a computer budgeting program, got night sweats wondering how we'd manage. We could feel our belts slowly tightening as our discretionary income dried up. Things that seemed like minor expenses when the babies first arrived, such as video rentals or fast-food runs, became luxuries to be appreciated as the months wore on. We began calculating how much food we could have purchased if we hadn't rented a movie.

Things didn't get too painful during the babies' first year, but I can foresee a day when they will be. Right now we do without little things, such as cable TV. But soon we may have to forgo not-so-little things. At least we have some experience at penny-pinching. Keith and I had some financial difficulties when I was pregnant, and we survived. Plus, our lifestyle keeps us thrifty. It's hard to spend too much money in restaurants when you never visit them, and tough to max out a credit card when you visit the mall maybe twice a year.

Though food will always be our biggest expense, school will run a close second. We will pay around six hundred dollars in book fees for our kids every year, then incur additional expenses for supplies and clothes.

Don't expect to see the Dilley family freely spending at The Gap every August to purchase the latest back-to-school fashions. Instead I'll find much of the children's everyday clothes at garage sales. About every six months we'll need a zillion new items, all in more or less the same size, all of which will become obsolete before the year ends.

An informal network of families with multiples may help defray some of these costs. The parents of some slightly older Indianapolis quadruplets pass on their kids' clothes to us as they outgrow them, and we pass on our things to a slightly younger set of local quintuplets. That arrangement helps immensely, but heaven help us when the kids get older and want to follow fashion. If they pine for fancy athletic shoes, Keith says he'll write NIKE on the sides of their sneakers.

At one time we thought that baby-product manufacturers would line up to use the Dilley sextuplets in commercials. But while we've been fortunate to have many necessities donated, including formula and high chairs, we long ago realized that endorsement money wouldn't put our kids through college.

We could have sought out such funds, but to get more cash we would have had to do things we didn't want to do. We would have needed an agent to shop the kids around, and we're not comfortable with putting the babies on an auction block. Our law firm deals with companies that approach *us*, but it doesn't aggressively seek out more business. We're simply not going to market the kids as if they were a product.

The babies have been in one commercial and a few print advertisements, but the opportunities are so erratic that we can't plan around them. Still, they do come in handy. Every time I begin to really worry, something comes through, be it a timely product donation or a small endorsement. It's just as well that we don't rely on this money, since we plan to stop most endorsements when the kids reach school age. We want people to think of them as individuals, not as The Dilley Sextuplets. Once, someone joked that we should find out if the kids can sing so we could cut a Partridge Family–style album.

But even if we somehow landed the one million dollars that so many people think we already have, I doubt that it would change our lifestyle much. Either Keith or I would still work full or part time, to set an example for the kids. Keith will return to work in a few years, and I will switch to part-time hours and help out more at home. Keith is reluctant to give up what he calls "the dad thing," but I think he needs to spend more time with adults, before he forgets how to speak in complete sentences.

Even in these allegedly enlightened times, he still draws stares when he tells people what he does. The concept of a stay-at-home dad just doesn't compute. I got the same sort of response in Geneva, whenever I told people I worked at home.

"Oh, you have your own business?" they would say.

"No," I'd reply. "I have six kids."

Actually, I guess we *do* have our own business. Watching the babies is like running a day-care center—a day-care center where the kids never leave. By taking primary responsibility for running ours, Keith saves us a fortune.

At least taxes aren't a problem, nor will they ever be. Keith, however, thinks our tax returns look so odd that we're bound to be audited. While we claimed only two deductions on our 1993 forms, on our 1994 return we claimed *eight*. I can just see some IRS employee spilling his coffee when he saw that.

Most of our financial problems are of the day-to-day variety, but one huge hurdle does loom—college. We haven't planned for it much because at this point there isn't much we can do. Most of our money is used up by routine expenses, which means that, barring a windfall, we won't be able to save as much as we would like. When the big day comes, our kids will have to take advantage of

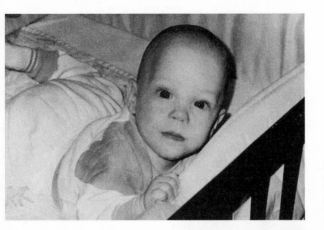

Quinn, early in the morning, with his cutest expression. He's trying to convince Becki to pick him up first.

Adrian with his own bunny and eggs on Easter

Claire with coauthor Sam Stall

every form of financial aid known to man, along with athletic and academic scholarships.

I also don't envision anyone going to Harvard, given the exploding costs of private universities. We'll favor state schools; the closer to home the college is, the better. Indianapolis has several universities, and if the kids are accepted there, they're welcome to spend their college years living at home. It will save a ton—even if it's not such a great party environment.

❀ 18 ❀

FUTURE SHOCKS

The children were all in a good mood, and we knew they were about to out-grow these outfits, so we took this photo.

❀ ❀ ❀ ❀ ❀ ❀

BECKI

A few weeks after the babies' first birthday I gave away the last of their six wind-up swings. They'd been a godsend during Keith's first days as a house husband, but now they were too small. It made perfect sense to pass them on to someone else. So why did my eyes tear up when the new owners loaded the last one into the back of their pickup and drove away?

I cried because everything was happening too soon. The sleepers, the swings, the bibs, all the trappings of the babies' first year seemed suddenly irrelevant, ready to be discarded and forgotten. *They* were ready, but *I* wasn't.

At about the same time I also boxed up most of the kids' first-year clothes and gave them to other families. I became sentimental about the strangest things. For some reason I couldn't part with their hats. I kept six Santa Claus caps from their first Christmas, along with beanies that matched a set of long-discarded rompers. They seemed impossibly small. Were the babies *ever* that tiny?

Of course they were, and not that long ago, either. Time seems to play tricks on me and Keith. We're so busy with day-to-day tasks that we rarely think beyond the next meal. For us, long-range planning is worrying in August about whether we have enough flannel sleepers for October.

But occasionally, in the midst of diapering and feeding and cleaning, we'll notice the calendar and realize another month has passed. That feeling hits hardest when I gather up a load of the children's discarded things—a bittersweet task that I'll face many times in the coming years.

Though we don't dwell on that distant future, sometimes Keith and I can't help thinking about it. Once we toured a church we hoped to attend when the babies got older. I said, "Can you imagine one day walking Brenna or Claire down this aisle?" Keith just looked away and said, "Let's not talk about it."

Fine with me. Worrying about such things will give us gray hair. Plus it violates one of our most sacred parenting rules: Live for today, savor every moment with the kids and don't waste time worrying about tomorrow.

We take comfort in the fact that most of the children's milestones are still far away—including some *really* alarming days, such as June 25, 2009, when all six get their driver's licenses. I'm also not quite ready to think about how we'll manage their after-school activities. We may mount a blackboard on a kitchen wall and have each child post his or her weekly schedule so we can determine who needs rides where. In spite of such precautions, I'm certain that someone will someday wind up stranded in front of their school in the rain with a tuba.

Those days will come sooner than we'd like, if the coming years pass as quickly as the last one. Twelve months ago the babies couldn't even turn over on their own, but today they're only a month or two away from learning to negotiate the stairs, which will open up the whole house to them. The thought of all six having the run of the place gives me the shakes. How will I feel a few years from now, when they all head out the door on Saturday night for dates?

Though that transition will be rough, it will be a piece of cake compared to the day when they move out on their own. I don't know how we'll survive after the kids leave. After so many years of scheduling our days to the minute, what will we do when the house falls silent and our time once again becomes our own? Maybe we'll go on a cruise or return to school—but only after we work through the empty feelings we will undoubtedly have when the last of the children moves out to be on his or her own.

Still, as Keith sometimes reminds me, having the kids leave home isn't the worst thing that could happen: Having them hanging around when they're thirty is. The kids will certainly be welcomed home if they fall on hard times or need a place to regroup, but I don't foresee a lack of ambition for this group. They'll be too busy running the world.

It's a bit early in their lives to predict their career paths, but here goes: Brenna will be a doctor and a devoted mom, because she loves people; Claire will become a veterinarian, because while she doesn't necessarily love *people* all the time, she adores animals; Quinn will be a business tycoon who makes million-dollar decisions but remembers to call his parents; Adrian (after four years as a starting offensive lineman for Notre Dame) will either become a member of the clergy or a social worker, where he can use his natural warmth and empathy; Ian, with his introspectiveness, will be an artist or musician; and Julian, who's always laughing, will be a standup comedian or entertainer.

That's about all the thought I can give to the kids' distant futures, at least without contracting a case of the blues. Right now, I can't wait for them to start talking. The babies lag behind other infants in this area, largely because they spend so much time together. They enjoy an almost psychic bond. A gesture or a glance can speak volumes, so there's little need for language. They've developed their own playroom civilization, and our job over the coming months is to help them join the human race.

Other moms whose kids already talk say I shouldn't be so anxious for them to master language. When they do, we'll probably need earplugs to cope with the noise. And what if they start chanting things, like "We're hungry"? It could be like a prison movie, with the inmates raking their tin cups over their cell bars.

While we work hard to help the kids learn, Keith and I also realize how much they've taught us. Coping with the babies forced us to take hold of our finances, and made Keith more outgoing, patient and organized. As for me, I think I've become less uptight, more patient and better able to cope with the unexpected. That's good, because the unexpected is our daily bread.

Other parents love to hear our war stories, though they rarely ask our advice. Tending six babies is so different from caring for one that few of our tactics apply to them. Parents of multiples quiz us, however, in part because there's so little literature on the subject. There are books on how to feed and bathe babies, but nothing on how to manage three or four at once.

That lack of information surprises me, given the recent explosion in multiple births caused by the wide use of fertility drugs. We'd love to add to the knowledge base by having a psychiatrist or anthropologist study our kids' behavior. Besides giving us new insights into their personalities, it might advance the understanding of multiples in general. But so far no one has stepped for-

Adrian with his own individual birthday cake. Each child got a cake, and each one dove into it.

The birthday party celebration. This was the first time the children were out in public and able to run around.

Their first party bags

ward. I think the goings-on in the playroom are a doctoral thesis or two waiting to be written.

Our special practical problems, such as how to bathe six babies, may not apply to the general public, but some of the other things we've learned apply to mothers and fathers the world over. First and foremost, we've discovered that parents face a never-ending series of goodbyes.

In a way, the kids have been leaving ever since we brought them home from the hospital. The fragile premies we tended so carefully are gone. So are the squirmy babies who first learned to crawl on Keith's dad's living-room floor. They've been replaced by a pack of rowdy toddlers, who will soon be replaced by kinder-gartners, then grade-schoolers.

I have six kids, yet I'll only experience these milestones once. That's why packing away their things is so hard. Another portion of the kids' lives, of our lives together, is gone. They don't need bottles anymore, they don't need wind-up swings, and one day they won't need us to fix all their problems, either. That, perhaps, is the toughest lesson any parent can learn.

So I save things—little shards of their lives that become touch-stones for my memory. I kept the clothes the babies came home in, along with some other outfits. I tell Keith that Claire and Brenna can use them as doll clothes someday (provided they can find them, since they're buried in the deepest corner of the master-bedroom closet). I have the scrubs Keith wore in the delivery room, along with the tiny arm cuffs used to monitor the newborns' blood pressure.

If I keep adding items at my present rate, someday we'll need an addition to hold them. But while I pack away school play programs and report cards, Keith and I hope the kids will start a collection of their own. We want them to collect one of the most priceless gifts parents can give: memories.

We can't give our children every material possession, but we'll give them all the love, discipline, attention and understanding they could ever want. When the kids finally leave home, they will depart with warm remembrances of family Christmases, Thanksgivings, school plays, Little League games and long summer days spent doing nothing. Wherever they go and whatever challenges they face, they will always remember a place and a time when they were safe and sound and loved.

Time flies, but those memories will last forever. I won't always be able to hold Julian, but he will *remember* how I once did. And Keith won't always be there to comfort Brenna, but she will *remember* that he once was. Whenever Keith and I visit the playroom, we mint new memories. We want them to be the best, because someday that's all we'll be.

A long time ago, when the babies first came home from the hospital, I sometimes longed for the day when they finally slept through the night. But I quickly stopped myself. I didn't want to wish any part of our children's lives away. That's even more true today, as I struggle to remember that long-ago time when I could hold Adrian in one hand and the kids actually *wanted* to be cuddled and rocked endlessly.

No one feels the passing of time like a parent, because the growth of a child reveals it far more poignantly than any clock or calendar. That's why we refuse to dwell on it. The future, we've learned, comes soon enough, no matter what we do.

But it's not here *yet*. Right now the babies are still in their playroom, squawking, running around and getting into trouble. Right now the babies' world revolves around us, and there's no danger we can't shield them from. Right now their whole lives—and our lives together—lie ahead of them. Right now we're far too busy having fun to get misty about the distant future.

And right now, we realize, will always be the very best time of all.

❋ 19 ❋

DILLEY RULES

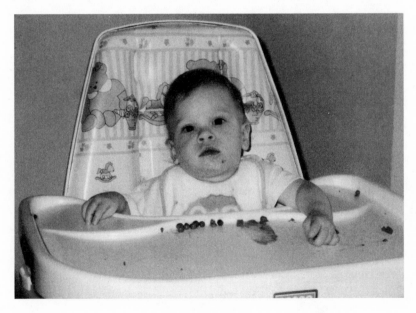

Julian, stuffed

❀ ❀ ❀ ❀ ❀ ❀

KEITH

With more than a year of practical experience, Becki and I consider ourselves two of the world's foremost experts on the care and feeding of sextuplets. In the unlikely event that this strange development becomes more common, we would like to offer the following tips for future parents of sextuplets.

1. If they're happy, *you're* happy . . .
One of the best things about sextuplets is that you don't have to constantly entertain them. A group of kids this large will find ways to amuse themselves. When they're content, don't do anything to mess it up. Just sit back and enjoy the relative silence.

2. . . . and if you're happy, *they're* happy.
The kids pick up on our moods. If we're late for an appointment and rushing around, they get just as nervous and upset as we do. On the positive side, the kids will bear almost any accidental

bump or bruise without crying if we simply smile and reassure them. If we're not worried, they're not worried.

3. Never forget you're outnumbered.

There are some things we can't stop the kids from doing, just because there are six of them and only two of us. For instance, several months ago they began knocking their cereal bowls onto the floor, then picking up the cereal bits off the carpet and eating them. Rather than spend every morning fighting this, we dumped cereal directly onto the playroom carpeting and let the kids go after it like pigeons after popcorn. It doesn't *look* great, but it gets the job done.

4. Empty the diaper pail. Now.

Diaper pails are nasty under the best of conditions. But when you change 36 to 48 diapers a day, like we do, they quickly become as toxic as Superfund sites. Ours crouches in the corner of the boys' bedroom closet. There's never a time when the pail is merely "full." It goes directly from "almost full" to "overflowing." To avoid this problem, we (meaning, "I") empty it every day. Otherwise it quickly transforms into a fragrant horror that Becki calls The Leaning Tower of Diapers.

5. Get help.

During Becki's pregnancy, friends and family members volunteered to assist us when the babies arrived. Usually we'd just smile and say something like, "Thanks, we'll get back to you." Now we realize we should have written down their names and phone numbers and compiled a card catalog. Becki and I pride ourselves on handling the kids solo, but those names might have come in handy when we needed emergency backup.

Just remember that sometimes the "help" isn't very helpful. People unaccustomed to handling premies may be so frightened by the babies' fragility that they freeze. Others may be so unfamiliar with child care that they slow *you* down with constant questions. Know people's strengths and weaknesses before asking for help.

6. Get earplugs.

Becki and I both think we've suffered hearing damage from facing six crying babies at once. Becki read that a crying child puts out something like a hundred decibels of noise. Multiply that by six, and you'll understand why we can't hear the TV quite as well as we once did. You absorb as much sonic punishment hanging out with our kids as you do at a heavy-metal concert—and your chances of getting puked on are about the same.

7. When it comes to diapers, you get what you pay for.

You know how diaper commercials go on endlessly about "flexible gathers that keep moisture in"? Well, trust us, this *matters*. Inexpensive brands lack elastic around the leg holes, which means they're prone to messy leakage. Cheap diapers cost less, but you spend the savings on extra detergent to wash poop-stained clothes, sheets and bed covers.

8. If pants don't have snaps, they stay in the store.

For parents with only one child, pants with legs that snap on instead pulling up over the legs are a convenience. For us, they're the difference between dressing the kids in ten minutes and dressing them in twenty. We do own a few "standard" pairs, but usually only one child wears them at any one time. Our worst piece is Claire's dreaded overalls. Not only don't they snap, they also include a bib and shoulder straps that are fastened by the most fiendishly unhandy buttons ever designed.

9. Kids travel best when they're tired.

We usually start all-day car excursions at nap time (around ten A.M.) so that the kids will sleep through the trip. Then we return at bedtime, so they'll sleep all the way home. We rarely stay overnight anywhere, because the babies refuse to nap during the day and have a tough time sleeping through the night. They're like me: They want their own beds.

10. Take all those cute group photos before the kids learn to crawl.

So you want a shot of the babies lined up on the couch wearing matching Santa outfits or bunny suits? Well, take them during their first six months, when they possess the mobility of potted plants and *have* to stay where you put them. Once the kids learn to move on their own, forget it. You'll be lucky if you get all six in the same frame, let alone smiling or looking at the camera. Be prepared to burn an entire role of film to get one decent shot.

11. Sextuplets love pets the way teenage girls loved The Beatles.

Dogs normally give babies a wide berth, but that's often impossible with our kids. If they see a pet, they surround and mob it the way girls go after rock stars. Once the kids cornered Becki's mom's fox terrier. Outnumbered and overstimulated, it sat in a corner, whimpering and terrified, as six toddling giants rubbed its head. The dog didn't dislike the kids and the kids didn't hurt the dog— it was just too much for the poor animal.

Though six kids would drive even the most patient dog batty (which is why we no longer have Winston), cats find ways to cope. They don't tolerate the kids any better; they just know how to escape. Take Ed. If the kids are upstairs, he's downstairs. And if the kids are on the east end of the house, he's on the west end.

12. Resist the temptation to dress them in matching outfits.

Sure it's cute. It's also, in our opinion, a bad precedent. Each child is unique, and it's unfair to lump them together so blatantly. Help them understand that they don't have to dress alike, act alike or think alike.

13. Being the center of attention isn't necessarily good.

All parents love being the most important thing in their children's world, but with six kids all that attention becomes inconvenient. For instance, whenever Becki or I walk upstairs to the playroom, the babies immediately rush the gate to greet us, making it impossible either to open the gate or step over it.

Other appeals for attention are far more subtle. When the kids first began eating solid food we watched them closely to make sure no one choked. As soon as the kids realized this, they began generating fake-sounding coughs while eating, then looking around at us to see if we paid attention to them.

14. Don't rock the kids to sleep every night.

Many child-care experts advise rocking babies just until they're sleepy, then putting them in their cribs to let them finish nodding off on their own. This is very important for sextuplets. If you rock them to sleep, then every time they wake up, including in the middle of the night, they'll expect the same treatment. Trust us: You don't have that much free time.

15. Practice teamwork.

Bystanders who watch Becki and me take the kids out of the van must think we're the most abrupt, brusque people in the world. While working, we seldom speak in complete sentences, confining ourselves to things like "Here" and "Grab that." We're not being short with each other; we just know what has to be done and exactly how to do it. Those curt instructions are the sounds of a well-oiled machine. Besides, we have to save our breath so we can . . .

16. . . . be ready to answer the same questions and listen to the same "witty" comments over and over and over again.

When the kids were babies, we heard the same questions everywhere we went: "Can you tell them apart?" "How old are they?" and "Are any of them twins?" As soon as they learn to talk, Becki and I hope to teach the *kids* to answer them. Even worse are the wits who serve us such classic bons mots as "Don't get much sleep, do ya," or "Oh honey, I feel sorry for you." Stop it, you're killing us.

17. Don't worry about postpartum depression.

Becki has a standard reply when asked if she felt depressed after the babies arrived. "Nope," she says. "No time."

18. Trust your gut.

In truth, there are no experts on how to raise sextuplets, and precious few who know anything about raising quads or quints. Just do what you think is right and realize you'll make mistakes. Also, some of the most practical solutions to caring for multiples seem nutty to people who have only raised one child at a time. For that reason, cut the general public some slack when they give you free—and useless—advice. They don't know, they *can't* know, how different raising multiples can be. Go your own way, trust your judgment, and do the best job you can.

19. Always remember how lucky you are that you were chosen to be uncommon parents.
Our days become so busy that sometimes we lose sight of the fact that we are such a major part of the unhurried lives of our children. Every day, something reminds us and touches our hearts: The sunrises are more radiant as we tiptoe into their bedrooms in the mornings. It is the joy of sharing in childhood discoveries again. And we find ourselves smiling and laughing more.

Always be thankful.

EPILOGUE

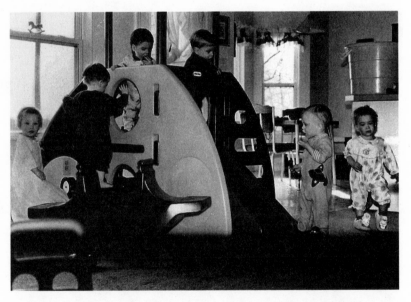

An afternoon of play on Valentine's Day, 1995. They're in sleepers because they've just been cleaned up after eating. Becki took the photo while Keith did his best to keep all of the children in the frame. Right now, this is their favorite toy because it gives them the opportunity to climb.

❀　❀　❀　❀　❀　❀

BECKI

The children changed quickly during their first year, but that was nothing compared to what's happened since.

It's late winter, 1995, and Brenna, Julian, Quinn, Claire, Ian and Adrian aren't babies anymore. They're tiny, toddling people with their own ideas about how to behave.

And, believe me, ever since the "terrific/terrible twos" arrived, it's been a challenge. For one thing, we can't seem to get ready on time anymore, no matter how early we start. In the good old days (say, seven or eight months ago) dressing the children was a breeze. We'd say, "Come to Mommy and Daddy," and they'd toddle over, smiling, and let us change their diapers and slip them into their outfits. No more. Now when we call, they scatter.

Usually we can't give chase, since we're both sitting on the floor, hemmed in by mountains of baby wipes, fresh diapers and six changes of clothes. Instead we must lure them to *us*, one after another. "Bring us a book, Claire," we'll say, and Claire will burst into a big smile, select one of her favorites and walk over to within grabbing range. Of course, we read her a few pages before changing begins.

A couple of months ago we switched to cloth diapers. It just became too expensive using disposable ones. Even generic brands were stretching our budget to the limit. We now wash one or two loads of diapers a day and it hasn't raised our water bill or our ire significantly. Besides, there's nothing better than the expression on Keith's face while he's rinsing diapers in the toilet. Now *that's* priceless.

The only problem with using cloth diapers is that it adds additional time to our already maxed-out schedule. Dressing and grooming the children used to take twenty to thirty minutes; now it seems to take forever. This means that Keith and I usually get the short end of the grooming stick. When we go out, the children look like they've stepped off a fashion runway, but Mommy and Daddy may look like they stepped in front of a truck. Once, when I took Brenna and Adrian to the pediatrician, I was so rushed that I didn't even glance at a mirror until I reached the doctor's office. Only then did I realize that I hadn't combed my hair or brushed my teeth, that my sweatshirt was covered with Desitin and I had poop on the cuff of my pants.

According to the dozens of baby books I've read over the past few months, the children are trying to define their personalities by resisting us. That's a polite way of saying they're occasionally impossible.

Discipline is a tough problem, especially since Keith and I have decided, for both philosophical and practical reasons, not to spank. These days a sharp "no" still suffices—except with Adrian, who for some reason won't heed verbal commands. He pays about as much attention to them as our cat Ed does.

Recently Adrian refused to quit messing with the stove controls, even after a series of ever-louder and more serious-sounding "nos." This couldn't continue, so the next time he did it I gave him yet another sharp "no," along with a smack on the offending hand. He instantly ran away and pouted in the corner, sucking his thumb and looking at me with tears in his eyes.

I planned to let him sulk for a few minutes, then pick him up and comfort him. But that wasn't what the *other* children had in mind. To my horror, Brenna and Claire marched over to Adrian, smacked his hands just as I had and said, "No, no, no." Then they smiled and looked past the now-hysterical Adrian for Mommy's approval. As I was comforting Adrian, I realized again just how tricky disciplining sextuplets can be.

While Claire is quick to discipline others, no one dares discipline *her*, for fear of retaliation. Yet she can also be incredibly sweet. A few weeks ago she learned to point at things and say, "What's that?" At first we laboriously identified everything she singled out, until we hit upon an answer she seemed to like even more. "That's *yours*, Claire," we would say, to her delight. The other children quickly noticed that Claire got attention with her questions, and now they all whisper, "What's that?" when we hold them.

Needless to say, the noise level at the Dilley household has increased dramatically. Our kids are probably behind other children their age in language skills, but that's fairly normal with multiples. When they *do* talk, they get lots of reinforcement from Keith and me, and we babble incessantly to encourage them. The children do their best to babble back, especially Brenna and Julian, though the monologue usually consists of saying, "Doi-doi-doi-DOI!-DOI!-DOI!-doi-doi-doi," at top volume for hours.

Adrian

Ian

Brenna

Julian

Quinn

Claire

Claire and Brenna are frequently the first to come up with new words, after which everyone copies them. They can say, "Hi, Daddy" and "Bye-bye," for instance. Usually the children only speak to Keith and me, though they'll say "no" to each other.

The children have made great strides physically. Adrian continues to grow like a weed, and though the others are still a bit small for their age, they're catching up. It was a bittersweet moment a few weeks ago when they finally lost their pudgy baby faces. Now they look like tiny adults. Interestingly, Julian, formerly the most delicate, has sprinted up the growth charts to become the second largest.

Though the kids are more rebellious now, getting attention, either from Keith and me or from their siblings, is still the name of the game. Quinn, a born clown who's always coming up with new tricks, still gets a lot of mileage out of jumping up and down in his crib. Adrian is our "door keeper," since he's the only one tall enough to manipulate doorknobs. And Julian, because of the position of his crib, scores a lot of points by incessantly switching the boys' bedroom light on and off.

The children are amazingly gentle with animals. While Ed (who misses his solo days) will have nothing to do with the children, our other recently acquired cats love them. Some might wonder why anyone tending six babies would want more pets, but Baby Bop (a gray-and-white longhair) and Ginger Snap (a former barn cat) fit in wonderfully. Every morning they come to the upstairs playroom gate to visit the children, and Baby Bop regularly leaps over the gate to mingle with them. She must have nerves of steel, because when the children spot her, they drop what they're doing and waddle toward her like zombies. After the children surround her in what Keith calls a "tiny rugby scrum," Baby Bop will pop out between someone's legs and walk away.

Riding herd on such antics keeps Keith and me occupied from dawn to dusk. We only *thought* we were busy when the children were newborns . . . yet I don't think our children are all that different from other kids their age. There's just *more* of them, which magnifies the good times and those Excedrin moments.

To keep them in their upstairs playroom, Keith removed the old pressure gate and replaced it with a much higher one that is mounted onto the walls with drywall screws. The only pressure gate still in use stands between the downstairs kitchen and the dining room, and its days are numbered. On any given day, two or three babies will grab on to it and pull in unison. They've gotten so good at this that they regularly pull it down.

They love pushing things around, or at least the things that aren't nailed down. In the upstairs playroom, their television is bolted to a dresser, and the dresser is bolted to the wall (Keith has become quite an expert with his power screwdriver). We once apprehended the boys as they tried to push one of their cribs through the bedroom door into the play area.

But none of these transgressions compares to the plundering of Keith's prized compact-disk collection. His only refuge from the children is his upstairs office, where he keeps his computer, the family records, books and dozens of carefully alphabetized CDs behind a closed door. Well, one day he forgot to shut the door, with predictable results.

Keith made the most amazing, high-pitched sound when he walked upstairs and found several of the silver discs unboxed and carelessly tossed over the playroom gate. I can imagine how he felt, based on previous CD-desecration incidents. Once, years ago, when Winston chewed up a ZZ Top disc, Keith stomped around for days saying, "That dog is gone. He's outta here."

That wasn't an option with the children, even though they wreaked far more havoc. The children slung perhaps a hundred CDs around the room, along with every book, file, and piece of paper they could lay their hands on. What could we do? Keith simply shooed everyone back into the playroom, cleaned up as best he could and closed the office door.

But for every crisis, there are six times as many occasions for joy.

Bath time, for example. We gather the children all together and herd them into our bathroom, which, thankfully, has an oversize tub. We strip them down and let them all lather up together. The laughs and screams of delight echoing through the bathroom are deafening, as the children splash about, pouring water on their toys. Lately, they have begun washing themselves and sporting shampoo hairdos. Keith particularly likes making the kids look like Ed Grimley. They would gladly play in the tub for hours.

Mealtime is actually getting easier. We replaced the high chairs with a plastic picnic table because the children would not stay seated in the high chairs. This turned out to be a blessing in disguise because it actually cut down on the mess. The children will eat just about anything that we put in front of them, and, thanks to baby teeth, we don't have to cut everything into tiny bits. Their favorite foods now include peanut butter and jelly, grilled cheese sandwiches and ravioli.

Playtime at the Dilley household remains action-packed. Our children perform stupid-human tricks that would be the envy of David Letterman. They will sing "Round and Round" while twirling about until they get so dizzy that they fall down. And, if their present skills are any indication, they have a bright future as furniture movers or band roadies. They'll push anything that isn't bolted to the wall.

Another activity that has become a crowd pleaser is reading. All Keith or I have to do is ask someone to bring us a book and we will end up with a lapful of children eagerly wanting us to read to them. Occasionally, they will even "read" to themselves and to one another, although the book might be upside down at the time.

Just like other parents, we have some very busy days when the work never seems to end and we sigh with relief as soon as the children are tucked into bed. And just like other parents, after they have fallen asleep, we will tiptoe in to check on them and look upon their faces. We forget any transgressions that have been committed throughout the day and fall in love with them all over again, still amazed by our special delivery.

We are ready for tomorrow.

ACKNOWLEDGMENTS

Our family would like to thank the staff of The Women's Hospital of Indianapolis for their knowledge, compassion and support. In particular we wish to thank Dr. David McLaughlin, Dr. Lynda Smirz, Dr. Belinda Watts, Dr. Betty Lou Walsman, Dr. Lydia Abad and Dr. Scott Curnow for their skill and belief in miracles.

We also want to thank the nurses at The Women's Hospital for their dedication, humor and loving support.

Special thanks to Karen for not letting us give up on achieving parenthood, and to Jane, whose support and guidance has made our lives so much easier.

Thanks to the support groups Resolve, Triplet Connection and MOST (Mothers of Super Twins).

At Random House, we are particularly grateful to publisher Harold Evans, Carol Schneider, Pamela Cannon, Amy Edelman, Linda Pennell, Miranda Brooks, Victoria Wong, Jennifer Eisenpresser, Andy Carpenter, and our editor, Jonathan Karp.

ACKNOWLEDGMENTS

Thanks to Sam Stall for his patience, energy and humor with us and the kids.

Finally, thanks to our families for all their patience and love; to our parents, whose wait for their first grandchild paid off six times over.

ABOUT THE AUTHORS

BECKI and KEITH DILLEY live in Indianapolis with their six children: Julian, Brenna, Claire, Quinn, Adrian and Ian.

SAM STALL is editor of *Indianapolis Monthly* magazine.

ABOUT THE TYPE

This book was set in Goudy, a typeface designed by Frederic William Goudy (1865–1947). Goudy began his career as a bookkeeper, but devoted the rest of his life to the pursuit of "recognized quality" in a printing type.

Goudy was produced in 1914 and was an instant bestseller for the foundry. It has generous curves and smooth, even color. It is regarded as one of Goudy's finest achievements.